"If you're looking for effective,
practical options for teaching your
children appropriate behavior,
you've come to the right place."
-Richard Carlson, author of
Don't Sweat the Small Stuff

Parenting
with Love & Limits

Jerry Wyckoff Phd
& Barbara C. Unell

"Treasured advice, new information, and explicit instructions
to help parents raise their children with love and limits."
-Marguerite Kelly, co-author of *The Mother's Almanac*

"A powerful tool that can help everyone who
reads it create a future in which children grow up
to become responsible, ethical and loving adults."
-Peter Yarrow of Peter, Paul and Mary; co-founder, Operation Respect

"As a mother, child advocate, and grandmother,
I know how important it is to get your whole 'parenting team'
(babysitters, teachers, relatives and close friends) on the
same page. This book shows you how to do it."
-Laura Kaiser, past president, Kansas PTA; vice-chair,
Communities in Schools of Mid-America

parenting *with* love & limits

jerry wyckoff, PhD
barbara c. unell

JAICO PUBLISHING HOUSE
Ahmedabad Bangalore Chennai
Delhi Hyderabad Kolkata Mumbai

Published by Jaico Publishing House
A-2 Jash Chambers, 7-A Sir Phirozshah Mehta Road
Fort, Mumbai - 400 001
jaicopub@jaicobooks.com
www.jaicobooks.com

Published in arrangement with
Meadowbrook Press
6110 Blue Circle Drive, Suite 237
Minnetonka, MN 55343, USA

To be sold only in India, Bangladesh, Bhutan,
Pakistan, Nepal, Sri Lanka and the Maldives.

PARENTING WITH LOVE & LIMITS
ISBN 978-81-8495-899-7

First Jaico Impression: 2017

Page design and layout: Auric Publishing, Mumbai

Printed by
Trinity Academy For Corporate Training Limited, Mumbai

This book is dedicated to our beloved children

Christopher Wyckoff, Alexander Wyckoff,
Julian Wyckoff, and Allison Wyckoff

Hieronymus Kasmai and Samira Kasmai

Justin Alex Unell, Leah Rachel Unell, and Amy Elizabeth Unell

Acknowledgments

"What's exciting about this opportunity is, we're at a tipping point in the development of this biological revolution we're living through in science – where we are now beginning to have a new understanding, in a way we never did before, of how early experience literally gets into the body and affects the development of the brain, affects the development of the cardiovascular system, the immune system, and metabolic systems."

Jack p. Shonkoff, MD, Director,
Center on the Developing Child, Harvard University

Our heartfelt thanks to all of the parents and parenting team members – as well as the social scientists, neurologists, developmental psychologists, and pediatricians – who have enriched our work through their passion for improving and protecting children's health and well-being.

Barbara is particularly grateful to Kathy Ellerbeck, MD; Steffany Barton, RN; and Laura Mead, for their generous energy and insight, which has been woven into the writing of this book. Barbara is also indebted to her lifelong friend Janice Benjamin and her dedicated medical colleagues at the University of Kansas Hospital: Cynthia King; Paul Arnold, MD; Tiffany Williams, MD; Jeremy Peterson, MD; David Smith, MD, FAAFP; Smith Manion,

MD; Sarah Johnson, RN, MSN; Melissa Smith, RN, MSN; Megan Bechtold, OPT, OC, CMPT; and Mary Suellentrop, DPT.

Finally, this book would not have been possible without the unwavering love of our kind and caring spouses – Millie and Robert.

Introduction

"When you hold your baby in your arms the first time,
and you think of all the things you can say and do
to influence him, it's a tremendous responsibility.
What you do with him can influence not only him,
but everyone he meets, and not for a day or
a month or a year but for time and eternity."
– Rose Fitzgerald Kennedy

Welcome to *Parenting with Love & Limits* – the revised, expanded, and retitled edition of our bestseller, *Discipline Without Shouting or Spanking*. We are gratified that over the past 30 years, *Discipline Without Shouting or Spanking* has helped hundreds of thousands of parents understand that shouting and spanking are counterproductive and damaging to a child's body, mind, and spirit.

We designed this book to cheer on today's parents and others caring for young children as they learn the skills to solve little ones' behavioral problems using calm, respectful words and actions. Our loving, practical approach to setting limits and building positive relationships makes both children and adults happier and healthier, as decades of behavioral and biological research have demonstrated.

In fact, we chose the title of this new book and the cover photo of a little hand gently touching a bigger hand because responsive, respectful nurturing of the connection between a caring adult and a young child is the most powerful predictor of a lifetime of good health, appropriate behavior, and success in school. Practicing discipline with love and limits with a child fosters a positive relationship, which promotes the following "dream-come-true" outcomes.

When you *discipline* a child, you *teach* her

- to take responsibility for her actions.
- to make decisions and solve problems.
- to handle mistakes as challenges, rather than disasters.
- to know the difference between appropriate and inappropriate behavior.

When you *love* a child, you share this powerful emotion through positive connections, and you

- create a respectful, safe, healthy environment built on mutual trust.
- accept and understand a child's inborn temperament and personality.
- respond calmly to inappropriate behavior instead of using punishment.

When you set behavioral *limits*, you set boundaries around your behavior and your child's, and you

- understand that threatening and violent forms of discipline are not options.
- become a role model of the appropriate behavior you are teaching.
- anticipate behavioral problems and try to prevent them before they occur.

To make this new edition even more valuable for families, and to respond to those who've asked us for help with new parenting challenges, we have included problem-solving strategies for these additional common behavioral problems:

- Bad Manners
- Bullying
- Car Travel Conflicts
- Climbing on Anything and Everything
- Cursing and Swearing
- Food Rules Conflicts
- Ignoring Requests
- Noise Problems
- Plane Travel Stress
- Too Much Screen Time
- Stealing

Another first for this book is our inclusion of life-changing research on the powerful impact that discipline has on the developing brain of infants, toddlers, and preschoolers. We have taken this data and translated it into new daily discipline strategies. Indeed, these game-changing findings add even more urgency to our longstanding zero-tolerance policy against shouting and spanking.

And there's more! In these pages, we present many easy-to-use, feel-good parenting strategies that will help everyone on your parenting team – Grandma, Grandpa, daycare providers, nannies, babysitters, preschool teachers, etc. – get along joyfully with your child. Practicing these good strategies together helps adults and young children build lifelong loving relationships.

As parents of adult children and grandparents of young children, we are honored that for decades we have helped families do the hardest, most important job on earth: disciplining children with love and limits by teaching them how to become responsible, self-sufficient adults. To help you do that, too, we have divided this book into easy-to-follow sections. Choose the section that meets your needs at any given moment:

- If you'd like to create a caring, supportive parenting team for your child, start with **Section One**.
- If you'd like to learn how to build positive, loving relationships between everyone on your parenting team and your child, start with **Section Two**.
- If you're curious about the latest brain research on discipline and how discipline affects lifelong health, start with **Section Three**.
- If you'd like a handy reference to terms used throughout the book, start with **Section Four**.
- If you need to solve one or more specific discipline problems, see the table of contents for the full list of

common childhood behavioral problems addressed in **Section Five**.

Parenting with Love & Limits is designed to be your go-to parenting resource during the beginning chapter of your family's life – and beyond. Your journey will be our journey as we nurture young children together.

Contents

Section One

Who Makes Parenting with Love & Limits Work?

You and Your Parenting Team

"The future of a society depends on its ability to foster the healthy development of the next generation."

—The Center for the Developing Child, Harvard University

Today, families with young children tell us that they need to use multiple arrangements of caring adults – what we call a parenting team – while they juggle raising their young children and going to work, caring for a young one while helping an aging parent, or enrolling a young one in an early childhood program and other enrichment activities (sports, for example). Regardless of the motivation behind having multiple people caring for children, this juggling act is a fact of life in parenting today: Millions of children under five years old spend at least one day a week in the care of someone other than their parents.

According to the United States Census, in a typical week during the spring of 2011, 12.5 million (61%) of the 20.4 million children under five years of age were in some type of regular childcare arrangement at least once a week. They were more likely to be cared for by a relative (42%) than by a non-relative (33%), while 12% were regularly cared for by both. Another 39% had no regular childcare arrangement.

The good news is that, as we've said before, all children need positive, loving relationships with caring adults. After all, it's these relationships that count the most! And caring adults can help children learn right from wrong and grow to be smart and healthy adults themselves.

So how do you get all of the members of your parenting team – relatives and non-relatives alike – on the same page so they can effectively be loving adults who set limits on your child's behavior and teach him how to get along with others in respectful ways?

WHO LEADS THE PARENTING TEAM?

Parents are, in effect, the parenting team captains, so parents are justified in respectfully helping everyone on their parenting team (babysitters, grandparents, daycare providers, and more) understand their personal parenting game rules – meaning how they want the team to care for the children. So we encourage parents to have frequent respectful discussions with everyone on their parenting team about the strategies in this book. This will let the whole team give children consistent messages about discipline rules designed to solve behavioral problems and build positive, loving relationships.

But it is also important to note that while parenting teammates may be happy to discipline a child with love and limits, some rules may change when a child goes to "play games" away from home – meaning when a child spends the day or night at different places. For example, the eating rules may be different at the child's home and the daycare home – or at one Grandma and Grandpa's house and the other grandparents' apartment.

So when those rules change – for example, when Grandma wants a child to stay up past her bedtime that she has at home – what are the parents' choices in response? First, it's important to stay cool and calm, not get angry and upset. A parent can tell herself, "My child understands that the rules may be different at Grandma Perkins's house – and that's okay." Children are capable of understanding and following different rules in different settings. After all, home rules and school rules are usually different, and children understand and abide by both as long as they have been taught that rules are important.

Ultimately, a parent needs to remember that she is the final decision maker. So if you're the mother or father, evaluate the difference between the rules at your house and at your child's Grandma's house or daycare, for example, and decide whether it is important to respectfully work with Grandma or the daycare provider to change their rules or not.

THE ONE EXCEPTION

On the other hand, rules about using violence – shouting, slapping, hitting, spanking, swatting, yelling, swearing, or doing anything else that could physically or emotionally harm your child – are NOT negotiable. For example, if your child's babysitter says that your child needs to be slapped because she has a sassy mouth, it's important to let that babysitter know that it is harmful to use any kind of violence in managing children's behavior. Let her know that your rule is to discipline without yelling or spanking – ever. Our discussion of toxic stress may help everyone on your parenting team understand the importance of your violence-free approach to raising children. (See Section Three, page 25)

RAISING CHILDREN AS A SINGLE PARENT

Parenting a young child alone – as sole caregiver for a certain number of days a week or all the time – is a difficult job for even the most skilled parent. Not only is parenting a 24-hour, seven-day-a-week job that requires patience, but it's also designed to be a team effort. So if parents are separated, divorced, or otherwise living apart, it is best if they work together to plan strategies, share duties, and decide on rules that will let them build independent, self-sufficient, loving, empathetic children. And instead of focusing on trying to control what the other parent does or doesn't do, each parent is best advised to use the strategies that we have outlined in this book. In this way, the child will receive discipline with love and limits from each parent.

Also, as stated previously, children are capable of understanding and following different rules in different settings because the rules are attached to the settings. It is important to note, however, that going to war with the other parent over child-rearing practices will result in the child's becoming collateral damage. No one escapes war without damage, so when parents cannot agree on rules, each parent needs to help the child understand that house rules may be different depending on which parent's house the child is living in at the time – and that it's okay for it to be that way.

If the other parent insists on using violence to discipline the child, and if you have exhausted reasoning with the other parent to bring about change, then you may seek legal intervention. Unfortunately, hitting children is not yet illegal in many places, so your only recourse may be to be a caring parent for your child and act as a buffer between your child and the other parent.

SPECIAL TEAM MEMBERS: When Emotions Run High Between Grandparents and Adult Children

The strength of the emotional relationship among grandparents, parents, and grandchildren can lead to conflicts around power and control over who's in charge when it comes to making decisions about discipline and parenting. Grandparents may think that they should be the bosses because they were always in that role with their children. They also may believe that their adult children should follow their lead when making parenting decisions because they are older and wiser.

Conflicts can also arise between generations over cultural changes, including what constitutes healthy eating. Parents may be tuned in to the health issues associated with diet and may demand that their children eat only organic foods, non-GMO foods, local farm-raised meat and produce, and gluten-free or dairy-free foods. Parents may require anything from Paleo to vegan diets for their children, but grandparents may follow simpler nutritional guidelines (for example, serving low-fat foods, low-sugar foods, etc.) that the children's parents have no interest in adopting for their little ones. Either way, meeting grandchildren's needs without alienating their parents requires a spirit of respectful compromise, conversation, and empathy to bridge the knowledge gap and keep mealtimes from becoming meltdown times. (See Mealtime Meltdowns, page 169)

Jealousy and competition can also cause friction between grandparents and their adult children, as well as between sets of grandparents. Although grandparents may not even realize that they have self-centered expectations about how their adult children should treat them, many keep score regarding how much time and what kinds of presents their grandchildren give to them and to their other grandparents. They may tell themselves things such as "My son should ask me to come over more. His wife asks her mom to babysit, but not me. And it's awful that my daughter never calls me anymore since she had her baby. And why do my son and his wife leave every time I come over to be with their kids?"

So if you are a grandparent and are upsetting yourself about your relationship with your adult children and your grandchildren, consider what this jealousy and scorekeeping is doing to your relationship with them – not to mention to your own stress levels. Ask yourself these questions:

- How is this helping me?
- How is this helping my children?
- What is my stress level when I say these hurtful things to myself?
- How is this helping my relationships with my children and grandchildren?
- Is this helping me be happy or miserable?
- What is the purpose of playing the "poor me" game?
- Is this the path to being the best grandparent I can be?

It's the messages that grandparents say to themselves that upset them. But when they change their self-talk to say that grandparenting small children and parenting adult children are not competitive games, they shift their mindset from a negative one to a positive one. They go from telling themselves "I want to be the favorite!" to "I am happy that my grandchildren have lots of relationships with caring adults."

All of these issues can be managed as long as you remain flexible and open to the needs of your grandchildren. After all, it's building the personal connections and positive relationships with your adult children and your grandchildren that is most important. Having battles over diets, formalities, and expectations will only prevent you from being the consistently caring grandparents that your grandchildren need you to be.

Section Two

How to Build a Positive Relationship with Your Child

While Working Together with Your Parenting Team

"If you are a parent recognize that it is the most important calling and rewarding challenge you have. What you do every day, what you say and how you act, will do more to shape the future of America than any other factor."

– Marion Wright Edelman, Founder, Children's Defence Fund

We marvel at the miraculous, ever-changing nature of human beings as they grow from wriggling infants into walking, talking whirlwinds of activity. As we focus on the practical, proven solutions to nurturing young children, it's important to first address children's complicated nature.

At their best, young children are curious, inventive, eager, and independent. At their worst, they are obstinate, inhibited, and clingy! Their chameleonlike personalities and inability to use adult logic make them tough customers when you're trying to sell them on life's most important behavioral lessons. And the irony is that the hardest time to build a positive, loving relationship with a child and to teach her appropriate behaviors is also the most important time to do so. That's because the earliest years of a child's life are her prime physical, emotional, and intellectual learning years. They are also precisely the time when children *need* to learn how to get along in the world: what they may do; what they may not do; and how to regulate their own responses when they get angry, frustrated, or fearful. That is what self-discipline really is all about.

Using the teaching approach to discipline with love and limits in this book to help children learn appropriate behavior builds a child's positive relationships with consistently caring, supportive, and protective adults – the sort of adults all children need in their lives in order to thrive.

Basic to this teaching system are the following strategies that you should encourage everyone on your parenting team to use every day while caring for your child.

BE EMPATHETIC

Empathy is the ability to identify with and understand another's situation, feelings, and motives – and it is the guiding principle of relationship-building strategies. All of us are born with the capacity to be empathetic. Research indicates that this ability varies from child to child as each one grows. Research also indicates that girls have a greater capacity than boys to read emotions. Nevertheless, by two years of age, both boys and girls are able to understand the feelings of others. By four years of age, children have the ability to comprehend the reasons for other people's feelings. However, if empathy is to grow and flourish in a child, adults must nurture its development.

The most important factor in building and maintaining empathy in a child is respecting her individuality by *modeling* empathy, understanding, and caring – regardless of how difficult her behavior may be to manage. For example, by beginning your response to inappropriate behavior with the statement "I'm sorry that you chose to do that," you're showing your child that you care about her feelings and have empathy for her being in the hot seat. In addition, parents can develop their child's potential to be empathetic by pointing out the impact of her behavior on others by asking "How do you think Andy feels when you push him out of the game?"

Conversely, reacting with anger to children's behavior erodes children's ability to be empathetic. When we react with anger, we also teach children to act without considering another person's feelings – a consequence we need to avoid. For example, studies have found that while greater maternal warmth is associated with increases in children's empathy during the second year of life, controlling children with anger is associated with decreases in children's empathy. Without empathy, it is nearly impossible for children to learn to share toys, play well with others, avoid angry and violent reactions to adversity, and take personal responsibility for their actions. But using the positive teaching strategies in this book will not only help keep your empathy quotient high, it will also help develop your children's potential to become empathetic, loving, caring adults.

Empathy also is a major factor in determining whether your child gets along well with others. Parents have experienced being upset and then being comforted by a young child who obviously understands their tears. Fostering empathy is very important in building that understanding, and having that ability to feel what others are experiencing helps your child be included in groups. It's a give-and-take reciprocal interaction. When your child behaves empathetically toward others in the group, she is more likely to receive empathy from others in the group and therefore receive the sense of safety and security such inclusion offers.

Young children who have empathy also develop a sense of fairness and the ability to generalize that fairness across their world. To a young child who has empathy, the idea that another child is excluded from the group because of skin color, language, size, or dress seems arbitrary and unfair.

BE PRESENT AND PAY UNDIVIDED ATTENTION TO YOUR CHILD

When giving your child undivided attention, make eye contact with her, talk to her, listen to what she says, repeat her words and phrases, guide her play, and be a trusted companion. Turn off the TV, smartphones, laptops, and other electronic gadgets - unless you are using them to watch or listen to a program together and discuss it with your child. Plan activities such as reading, singing, talking about your day, describing your child's activities to her, going on outings, or playing outside. Get down on the floor with your child so that she can see your face and know that you are there for her and her alone. All these are simple but profoundly important examples of ways to build a positive, loving relationship with your child!

If your job is home based, you may be telling yourself that you cannot spend all of your child's waking hours playing with her and giving her your undivided attention. We understand. However, you no doubt also understand how much chaos is caused when you close your office door and lock your child out while you work. Similarly, you know that the idea of putting up a gate on your office door so you can see your child but she can't reach you is also an invitation for frustration. So if you work at home, we believe that it is best for you to consider these choices:

- Enlist a friend or relative who is a trusted childcare provider.
- Find a suitable daycare, preschool, or early learning program that meets your and your child's needs.
- Work at home while your co-parent is available to take care of your child.
- Hire a babysitter or nanny to come to your home to take care of your child while you work.

Multi-tasking between work and childcare while at home may occasionally be doable; but as noted, it is a recipe for someone (you or your little one) to get angry, frustrated, and resentful. So figure out a strategy to meet your own agenda for paying attention to your work as well as your little one's agenda for getting attention from a caring adult. This will prevent behavioral problems. (See Think About How to Meet Both Your Agenda and Your Child's, page 17)

A Note About Ignoring Your Child's Need for Attention

In today's wired and wireless world, multi-tasking is the norm, with a constant bombardment of electronic noise demanding your attention. We all have become accustomed to this electronic noise, and as a result, we tend to focus on the most immediate noise while tuning out all else. When infants and young children are introduced into this mix, we can be so distracted that their "noise" becomes just another noisy distraction trying to pull us into their world. Babies are preprogrammed to become the greatest of noisemakers because their very survival depends on attracting the attention of a caregiver. As a result, babies can cry at the same decibel level as the noise from a jackhammer – a most annoying distraction when your attention is focused elsewhere! In addition, young children are naturally quite egocentric. They believe that they exist at the center of the universe and everything should orbit around them. So a young child who tries to gain a parent's attention will continue to try until, if no attention comes, she will be left with the dysfunctional choices of trying to fight for attention (e.g., have a tantrum, whine, name-call), threatening to run away, or making the cause of the stress (the parent) irrelevant by ignoring him when he finally does pay attention. When a parent ignores his child and thus becomes irrelevant to the child, the parent-child relationship becomes toxic because of the unhealthy physical reaction of the child's unrelenting stress level.

TALK AND READ TO YOUR CHILD

Talking and reading to your child is of vital importance in building your positive relationship with your child, as well as in helping her develop good behavior and social skills. The more words she knows, the more she can think – because she thinks in words.

Language is learned best in conversation with other people, rather than from TV or from listening to someone else's phone conversations. It's the one-on-one interaction that is the most important, not just the words. When you converse with your child using eye contact and positive, caring, respectful language, you are not just teaching her new words. You are building a caring relationship with her as well.

Landmark studies over the past 30 years have demonstrated the importance of language in building a child's future. These studies found a tremendous achievement gap between children who had a rich language experience during their early years and those who didn't. The number of words a child heard from birth made the difference. As a result, it turns out that conversing with and reading to your child are two of the most intimate and intellectually stimulating parts of being a parent.

You can even start this process during infancy, before your child can say words. Begin by imitating her sounds. If she is making mouth noises, such as "Ba, ba, ba," repeat those sounds so that she begins to understand that making sounds means connecting with a significant adult in her world. She will know that you are there and that you are holding a "baby conversation" with her.

Conversation can involve simply describing the activity in which you and your child are engaged. In the car, talk about what you are seeing – things like landmarks, people, and activities. In the supermarket, review your shopping list aloud, describing the items you are buying by their size, color, and weight.

Research on language development in children has discovered that the style of words used is also important. When talking to your child, use affirming words, such as "Good listening," or "Let's try it this way." Avoid using discouraging phrases, such as "That's not the way to do that," or "That's wrong." And when you must reprimand, state the desired outcome, such as "It's important to leave the dirt in the flowerpot so the flower can grow." Avoid just saying "No!" or "Stop that!"

The words you use will be used by your child, so keep them positive. When having any conversation with your child, get on her level physically so you can see each other. Talk to your child as an equal, the way you would to any adult you love and care about. Use the same language you would with another adult. That, of course, also means you must avoid using words that you don't want your children to use – curse words, for example. Even when you're not conversing with your child, we suggest that you avoid using such words within earshot of you child. Children learn powerful words, good or bad, and they quickly discover the meaning of those words from the context in which they are used!

INCREASE YOUR CHILD'S FRUSTRATION TOLERANCE AND ABILITY TO DELAY GRATIFICATION

One result of living in a world where we're connected to everyone and everything 24/7 is that we are frustrated and disappointed when we don't get immediate feedback to every text, tweet, social media post, or phone call. When we lack frustration tolerance and the ability to delay gratification for ourselves, it's hard to teach our children the virtue of patience.

So begin the process by practicing patience yourself. For example, when you're stuck in traffic with your young child safely strapped in a car seat, don't fume at a stoplight or yell at other drivers to hurry up. That sets the standard for your child when she wants something immediately. When you yell and fume, she learns from you that when she's frustrated, anger is appropriate and yelling is coping. Those are two lessons you don't want her to learn! Instead, model your ability to delay getting what you want and keep your frustration in check by saying "The traffic is really heavy today, but we can sing songs and make it fun while we're waiting for the traffic to move."

You can help build your child's frustration tolerance and ability to delay gratification by taking small steps like delaying delivery of what your child wants for a few seconds at first and then gradually extending the time until the payoff. This teaches her that what she wants will eventually be there. Talking to her while she waits will further build her frustration tolerance and give her words she can use to help herself in the future. Saying things such as "We can get a snack when we have put the blocks in the box," (see Grandma's Rule, page 37) tells your child that there is value in doing what needs to be done before doing what she would like. Longitudinal research has found that children who learn to delay gratification when they are young have better chances of becoming patient, trustworthy adults.

When you promise your child that patience will pay off, you tell her that she can depend on you when you say you will do something. This is another way of demonstrating that you are a caring adult. It will help your child be more willing to delay her own gratification and trust that the payoff will come in time.

THINK ABOUT HOW TO MEET BOTH YOUR AGENDA AND YOUR CHILD'S

All children, especially young children, have tantrums, whine, and do all or most of the 43 behaviors we explore in Section Five of our book. They do this no matter how perfect their parents might be! Both well-adjusted and not-so-well-adjusted children of every socioeconomic background have needs and wants, as do their parents and other adults who care for them.

Problems arise when the needs and wants of parents and children don't fit together like pieces of a puzzle. Parents want to have the power to be able to control their child so their own agenda can be met. Conflict develops when their child also seeks power and control to meet her own agenda.

For example, conflict will develop when you want your child to get dressed and her agenda is to play. You may want to exercise the power you believe you possess as a parent, but she wants to control her own agenda. Depending on the strength of what you're telling yourself about the need for you to have the power in this situation, the conflict can escalate or it can be resolved.

So instead of telling yourself that you must have control, you can resolve this conflict by telling yourself that you don't need to overpower your child to meet your own agenda. Just say, "I understand you want to continue playing instead of getting dressed. But we need to get ready to go to school, so I would like your cooperation." This calmly validates your child's agenda while letting her know about yours. Use what we call Grandma's Rule (see page 37) by telling her "When you get dressed, then you may play until we need to leave. You are so good at getting yourself dressed." By understanding both your and your child's needs, you can resolve the power-control conflict and thereby gain your child's cooperation.

Conflicts over agendas are major sources of stress for parents and young children. When these conflicts become chronic because an adult doesn't resolve them with love and limits, they can trigger a harmful stress response that does not abate. This stress response can become toxic and damage your child's emotional and physical health now and in the future. (See Section Three, page 25)

SEPARATE YOUR OWN SENSE OF SELF-WORTH FROM YOUR CHILD'S BEHAVIOR

"Oh, you won't believe how smart Suzy is. She just amazes me. She is such a genius."

How many times have you heard such statements from friends and acquaintances? Maybe you have said similar things about your own child. It is important to be excited about your child's skills and abilities and to encourage the development of those skills. Your child needs your support, but bragging to your friend or neighbor may be a slippery slope if you do it within earshot of your child. Why? When your child becomes part of your "I'm a successful parent," resume, she will come to believe that she controls your happiness. If she succeeds and meets your expectations, then you will be happy with her. However, if she fails, then you will be unhappy with her. This is a dangerous position for your child to be in.

It is important to separate yourself from your child. First of all, you don't have any control over her skills or abilities or even her desire to use those skills. But you do have control over the words you say and how you act, as well as how the parenting team responds to your child's behavior. And that is where to put your effort.

It is also important to separate your child from her behavior. She is, after all, not her behavior. She is a child, a person. Her behavior is what she does as a child. It is not who she is. She is a kid who plays soccer, for example. Thus, what she does – like playing soccer – can be changed. But who she is cannot.

You and your parenting team need to accept your child, but not always her behavior. If she acts out at the supermarket, it is only her behavior that's annoying, and that can be changed. She is neither a good nor a bad child, and her behavior is not you, even though you may be saying to yourself "My child is bad, and that makes me a bad parent." It's the behavior that you want to change, not the child.

So your parenting resume can certainly include your child but not your child's successes or failures. What needs to be on your resume is that you share loving connections with your child and are teaching your child the limits that are appropriate for her behavior and that will stand her in good stead as she grows and develops.

Protect Your Child Against Victimization (Bullying, Verbal Abuse, Physical Abuse, Sexual Abuse, etc.)

One of your most important responsibilities as a parent is to protect your child from becoming a victim while in your care, as well as while in the care of others on your parenting team – including babysitters, daycare providers, teachers, and family members. To do this, you need to perform two jobs. First, before you enroll your child in a daycare or preschool program or hire a nanny or babysitter, make sure the person or people who will be responsible for your baby's or child's safety and well-being are committed to protecting your child from harm.

Second, teach your young child things she can say to help protect herself, such as the following:

- "I don't like it when you do that. Please stop."
- "I don't know you, so I can't go with you."
- "Stop throwing sand at me."

Once you have decided on what protective statements you want to teach your child, practice with her by playing the Pretend Game. Say, "Pretend we are playing in the sand and I am throwing sand at you. What are you going to say?" You may prompt and encourage your child until she says what you have taught her to say. Then praise her effort and try another scenario.

To help determine if your child is being bullied when you are not around, check this list from Stopbullying.gov. Some signs that may point to a bullying problem are as follows:

- Unexplainable injuries
- Lost or destroyed clothing, books, electronics, or jewelry
- Having frequent headaches or stomachaches, feeling sick, or faking illness
- Changes in eating habits, like suddenly skipping meals or binge eating (e.g., coming home from school hungry due to not eating lunch)
- Difficulty sleeping or frequent nightmares
- Declining grades, loss of interest in schoolwork, or not wanting to go to school
- Sudden loss of friends or avoidance of social situations
- Feelings of helplessness or decreased self-esteem
- Self-destructive behaviors, such as running away, self-harm, or talking about suicide
- New signs of aggression to animals or people, such as hitting or biting

If you see these symptoms, have a conversation with your child about why they may be occurring. Ask open questions that can't be answered by a simple yes or no. Don't say, "Does your stomach hurt?" Instead, say, "I think you are acting like your stomach hurts. Sometimes when my stomach hurts, it's because I am worried about something. Tell me what you're worried about."

Depending on the situation, you may choose to get help determining the root of these symptoms from healthcare providers, school resources, and others close to your child or on your parenting team. And once you know if bullying is the cause of your child's distress, the next step is to begin working with those in your community who oversee the protection of children to help you solve this problem.

UNDERSTAND THE DIFFERENCE BETWEEN BOYS AND GIRLS

Note: The discussion below contains broad generalizations based on the vast amount of research on the development of boys and girls. Individual children may vary from these tendencies. However, this information can help you distinguish between normal behaviors and those that need to be addressed as problems. Knowing the natural differences between boys and girls can also help you avoid comparing your different-sex children to each other. Also see Appendix I: Milestones of Healthy Childhood Development, page 280, for information on the developmental stages of young children.

To build a positive relationship with your child, it's helpful to understand that boys and girls differ not only in physical structure but also in brain structure, body chemistry, and hormones. These differences strongly influence boy-girl behavior dissimilarities.

For example, in utero, boys' brains develop more slowly than girls' brains. In boys, the left half of the brain, which controls thinking, develops more slowly than does the right half, which controls spatial relationships. Also, the connection between the hemispheres is slow to develop. As a result, boys generally enjoy greater ability in math and reasoning but lesser ability in language and reading.

Girls' brains develop more evenly, with the hemispheres firmly connected. This gives them the ability to use both hemispheres for such things as reading and emotional awareness. The female brain is at work most of the time, allowing girls to be more skilled at multi-tasking. Girls' bodies also secrete more serotonin, a neurotransmitter that inhibits aggression.

On the other hand, boys' bodies secrete more testosterone, a hormone that drives aggression. As a result, boys tend to seek instant gratification (eating quickly and jumping from activity to activity), move quickly to problem solving (even in highly emotional situations), and engage in activities that create tension (sports, contests, and games). These tendencies allow boys to release testosterone-driven pent-up energy.

Other common differences between boys and girls include the following:

- Boys prefer to focus on a single task, and they react more aggressively to interruptions.
- Girls' motor activities peak less quickly, are more vigorous, and last longer.
- Boys create and play games that fill larger spaces. They therefore need more space for themselves and need to be outside more.
- Girls' attention to objects is less fleeting and less active.
- Girls rely more on their five senses: smell, hearing, taste, vision and touch.
- Boys do better with visual information presented to the left eye – which feeds into the right hemisphere of the brain, their stronger hemisphere.
- By age five, girls are six months ahead of boys in general development.
- Boys who see themselves as physically strong will seek rough-and-tumble play.
- Boys who feel safe and competent will seek independence earlier than will girls.

Section Three

Why Parenting with Love & Limits Works

New Research on Spanking, the Brain, and Emotional and Physical Health

"We see how early childhood experiences
are so important to lifelong outcomes,
how the early environment literally becomes
embedded in the brain and changes its architecture."
– Andrew Garner, MD, PhD, FAAP

In the United States, 78% of fathers and 66% of mothers believe that a child sometimes "needs a good, hard spanking." Amazingly, 15% of babies are spanked before their first birthday.[1]

These statistics motivate us to give you, in startling detail, the profoundly important scientific research findings about the impact of using any kind of violence – spanking, swatting, slapping, hitting, or threatening – as discipline. We have all heard these justifications for why a person spanks a child:

- "I've got to give my child a good spanking to get him to do what I say!"
- "I love my child, but I have to spank him for his own good."
- "Sometimes my child needs to be spanked."
- "My parents spanked me when I did something wrong, so I need to spank my child."
- "I had to spank him for hitting his brother!"
- "I had to hit my child to get his attention."
- "I spanked my child because I didn't know what else to do to make him stop."

Not only are these justifications harmful, but apologizing for spanking a child by saying "I'm sorry, I only hit you because I love you," or "This hurts me more than it hurts you," or "What you did made me have to spank you," also damages a child's emotional health. Why? Because these so-called justifications for using violence send the message to the child that he is not worthy of being loved and protected and that it's okay to hit someone you love to shape him up. These are not messages that parents want to send to their child - ever - so apologizing for spanking can be just as emotionally damaging as the spanking itself can be.

SPANKING IS BULLYING

In simple terms, spanking is actually a form of bullying. *Bullying* is defined as follows: to treat in an overbearing or intimidating manner; to make one's way aggressively; to force one's way aggressively or by intimidation; frightening, terrorizing, blustering, or domineering.

When someone hits or yells at a child – just as a bully would – the child will fear that person so much that he will do what the person wants him to do, just to stop the pain and anxiety that he is experiencing. Hitting, slapping, using abusive language, and making threats of spanking may seem to work because they produce these immediate results – but at what cost to a child?

THE IMPACT ON A CHILD'S BRAIN

This is what happens when a child experiences violence: the bullying behavior triggers a fear response that arouses an autonomic, built-in physical reaction, and a child will do what the adult wants just to "put out the fire" of the stress reaction in his brain and body. The sequence of the stress response looks like this:

1. An adult threatens or actually spanks, swats, or slaps a child.
2. The child perceives this action as a threat.
3. The fear part of his brain says, "DANGER!"
4. His body and brain react to this danger with a fight-or-flight response, telling him he must either hit back or run away.
5. The fight-or-flight response causes his blood pressure to increase, his heart rate to go up, and his stress hormones (e.g., Cortisol) to increase. This stress reaction also causes other physical changes – including changes to his brain.

Stress psychologists have found a biological explanation for this. The part of the brain most affected by stress is the prefrontal cortex, which is the decision-making part of the brain. So children who grow up in stressful environments – including environments in which they are spanked – generally find it harder to concentrate, sit still, rebound from disappointment, and follow directions. And above all, they find it harder to self-regulate, meaning to exercise self-control.

In *How Children Succeed,* Paul Tough reports the following: When kindergarten teachers are surveyed about their students, they say that the biggest problem they face is not children who don't know their letters and numbers; it is kids who don't know how to manage their tempers or calm themselves down after provocation. In one national survey, 46% of kindergarten teachers said that at least half of the kids in their class had problems following directions. In another study, Head Start teachers reported that more than a quarter of their students exhibited serious self-control-related negative behaviors, such as kicking or threatening other students, at least once a week.[2]

And there's no shortage of other alarming statistics about the effects of spanking on children's behavior and health: a meta-analysis of 88 scientific studies over 62 years found a remarkable 94% consensus that spanking is significantly associated with the following undesirable behaviors and experiences:[3]

- Decreased moral internalization
- Increased child aggression – defined as argumentative, disobedient, and cruel behavior; destroying things, physically attacking people, and screaming
- Increased child delinquent and antisocial behavior
- Decreased quality of relationship between parent and child
- Decreased child mental health

- Increased risk of being a victim of physical abuse
- Increased adult aggression
- Increased adult criminal and antisocial behavior
- Decreased adult mental health
- Increased risk of abusing own child or spouse
- Increased drug and alcohol abuse

All of these behaviors are related to the functioning of the prefrontal cortex and its importance in regulating impulses, including a child's moral development. According to psychologist Lawrence Kohlberg, the lowest level of moral development is "following rules only to avoid punishment. The highest level is following rules because they are right and good."[4] When parents spank their children for misbehavior, they stop their children at the lowest level of moral development. The children are interested in avoiding the punishment, not in doing what is good or right.

WHY SPANKING DOESN'T WORK: More Bad News About Spanking

Spanking as punishment simply drives bad behavior underground. It stops the behavior from happening in front of a parent, but it doesn't stop it altogether. In fact, children who are spanked become experts at not getting caught. Parents may say, "Don't let me catch you doing that again," and children will make sure they don't.

At times, you may find yourself operating on this level to avoid punishment! Let's say that you are driving above the speed limit and see a police car. What do you do? Your reaction may be the same as your child's: just hide what you're doing so you don't get caught. You'll slow down, behaving appropriately while in view of the police car, and then resume speeding after the police car is out of sight. That's acting at the lowest level of moral development.

But when you drive the speed limit all the time, you are driving according to the highest level of moral development.

On the other hand, the meta-analysis quoted above revealed that spanking is associated with only one desirable behavior, as we've noted earlier in this section: increased immediate compliance. It also noted that adults who were spanked as children have more stress-related health problems, including an increased chance of developing these physical conditions:[5]

- Hypertension
- Hepatic disease
- Diabetes
- Cardiovascular disease
- Gastrointestinal disease
- Arthritis
- Obesity

SEEK PROFESSIONAL HELP

If you or your parenting team members simply cannot stop using spanking as a method of disciplining your child, we urge you and them to seek professional help from a pediatrician or counselor. This can help stop your and their hurtful behavior from causing a toxic stress response in your child's health and brain. The term *toxic stress* is the formal term used by the medical and scientific community to describe the excessive or prolonged activation of the physiological stress response system in the absence of stable, caring relationships.[6] This kind of prolonged activation of stress response systems can disrupt the development of brain architecture and other organ systems, as we have noted, and it can increase the risk of stress-related disease and cognitive impairment well into the adult years.[7] (See Appendix IV, page 293)

THE LEARNED NATURE OF VIOLENCE

Studies of people who have been convicted of violent crimes show that their violent behavior was learned. They either witnessed violence inflicted on others or had violence inflicted on themselves. They learned that violence and power go together. And when children are spanked, slapped, punched, or even threatened with violence, they learn that big, powerful adults get their way through violent acts. The children, in turn, try to use violence to exert power over others.

The primary message parents send when they yell or spank is that adults are bigger, stronger, and more powerful than children and can inflict fear and pain if displeased. The children's resulting sense of being victims and being powerless in the face of greater size and strength creates fear, anxiety, and ultimately the desire to use violence themselves when upset. Children see the world in concrete terms, and when they see that it's permissible for adults to hit children, they assume it must be permissible for them to hit adults or other children. Hitting begets hitting – as well as anger, revenge, and the breakdown of communication between adults and children. It is the OPPOSITE of the behavior of a caring, supportive, and protective adult.

The United Nations Committee on the Rights of the Child defines physical punishment that causes any degree of pain and discomfort (even mild) as abuse. They argue that eliminating corporal punishment of children is "a key strategy for reducing and preventing all forms of violence in societies." They define corporal punishment as the use of "physical force with the intention of causing a child to experience pain, but not injury, for the purposes of correction or control of the child's behavior."[8]

We are in full agreement. Children learn to behave in violent ways through adult example – a compelling reason to avoid spanking, hitting, slapping, abusive language, threats of violence, or any other form or threat of physical or emotional pain. This is particularly important given the increased exposure children have to violence in the media. Research has shown that children who watch violence online, on TV, in movies, or in video games are more aggressive with playmates. Through the media, they are learning again that violence can give people power and that using violence is an acceptable way to get what they want. That's why we believe that it is vitally important for everyone on the parenting team to be aware of the dangerous consequences of the use of violence in any form, either threatened or actually inflicted on a child or another person or witnessed through media exposure.

As we have said in so many ways in this section, NO positive consequences result from spanking or yelling at a child (or anyone!). In fact, the link between the victimization of children and their subsequent anger management problems further underscores the argument for creating a zero-tolerance policy regarding spanking and threatening behavior in your home and your child's daycare, preschool, and other settings. This policy should be a statement of your own beliefs that discipline should be a teaching system that builds appropriate behavior through love and limits.

Therefore, we are as resolved as ever to ensure that all of those caring for children know what to do to teach a child appropriate behavior in positive ways. Doing so fosters healthy connections and loving relationships between parents and children. As author Barbara Fredrickson describes in her book *Love 2.0,* love, as our body experiences it, strengthens the connection between our brain and our heart and promotes children's and adults' physical, emotional, and psychological health.[9]

Notes

1. “The Psychology of Spanking,” Online Psychology Degrees, http://www.online-psychology-degrees.org/psychology-of-spanking/.
2. Paul Tough, *How Children Succeed: Grit, Curiosity, and the Hidden Power of Character* (Boston: Houghton Mifflin Harcourt, 2012).
3. “The Psychology of Spanking,” Online Psychology Degrees, http://www.online-psychology-degrees.org/psychology-of-spanking/.
4. Lawrence Kohlberg, *The Philosophy of Moral Development: Moral Stages and the Idea of Justice* (Harper and Row, 1981).
5. “The Psychology of Spanking,” Online Psychology Degrees, http://www.online-psychology-degrees.org/psychology-of-spanking/.
6. “Key Concepts: Toxic Stress,” Center for the Developing Child, Harvard University, http://developingchild.harvard.edu/key_concepts/toxic_stress_response/.
7. “Adverse Childhood Experiences (ACE) Study,” Centers for Disease Control and Prevention, http://www.cdc.gov/violenceprevention/acestudy/.

8. "Prohibiting and Eliminating Corporal Punishment of Children—A Key Element of State Responsibility for Eliminating Violence against Women and Girls," Global Initiative to End All Corporal Punishment of Children, http://www.endcorporalpunishment.org/pages/pdfs/submissions/Global%20Initiative%20submission%20to%20SR%20study%20on%20eliminating%20violence%20against%20women.pdf.
9. "Micro Moments of Love", Barbara Fredrickson, June 17, 2013, http://www.awakin.org/read/view. php?tid=949#sthash.zxlXP2tP.dpuf.

Section Four

Your Discipline Dictionary

A Quick Guide to
the Basic Vocabulary of
Disciplining with Love & Limits

"If the only tool you have is a hammer,
you tend to see every problem as a nail."
– Abraham Maslow

This section defines the basic vocabulary that everyone on your parenting team can use to solve the 43 most common childhood behavior problems listed in Section Five.

BEAT-THE-CLOCK

A motivational technique that uses your child's competitive nature to encourage him to complete tasks on your timetable. Set a timer (the timer on your smartphone is handy) for the amount of time you want to allow your child to complete a task. Then say to him, "Let's see if you can finish before the timer sounds." Since children love to win, this allows them to win a race against time. More importantly, your child will complete the task in a timely fashion without a power struggle, and the clock will act as the controller, instead of you.

Using Beat-the-Clock when you want your child to get ready for bed, for example, will help you reduce the child-adult conflict because you will be transferring the authority to a neutral figure – a clock.

CALM TIME

A set period of time for which an adult takes a child out of a situation because of the child's inappropriate behavior, in order to allow both the child and the adult to gain self-control.

One of the benefits of calm time is that it separates you from your child when tempers are flaring, giving you and your child the opportunity to calm down. However, if you rely only on calm time to stop inappropriate behavior and don't teach the behavior that you want during neutral time (see below), your child will continue to use the inappropriate behavior and thus spend most of his day in calm time!

A typical calm time involves taking your child to a chair or a room, setting your smartphone timer for a certain length of time (approximately one minute for each year of age, up to five minutes maximum), and telling him he needs to stay there until the timer sounds. If he leaves calm time before the timer sounds, reset the timer and tell him that he has to stay there until the timer sounds. Repeat the process until he stays in calm time for the designated amount of time.

When using calm time, say, "I'm sorry that you need to leave your play right now to calm yourself down." Then, in a caring manner, walk your child to calm time and say, for example, "Please stay here in this calm time to think about what you could do instead of hitting your sister when you are mad."

When calm time is over, ask your child "What do you think you could do so you can stay and play when you get mad?" Talk with your child about his answers. If he tells you "I don't know," or doesn't seem to have the words to describe his thinking, share some of your ideas, such as "Use your words instead of your fists," or "Go get an adult to help you when you are angry." Once you have finished talking with your child about ways to solve the problem, leave it to history and don't keep bringing it up. What's done is done. Working toward a better future makes more sense than dwelling on the past. Reminding your children of their errors only reminds them of what NOT to do and does not show them what you want them TO do.

GRANDMA'S RULE

A contractual arrangement that follows the pattern "When you have done X (what you want your child to do), then you may do Y (what your child wants to do)."

Grandma's Rule is best stated in the positive rather than the negative, as in "When you have done this, then you may do that," rather than "If you don't do this, then you can't do that."

NEUTRAL TIME

Time that's free from conflict, such as the time after a tantrum is finished and when your child is playing calmly.
Neutral time is the best time for teaching new behavior because your child is calm and therefore receptive to learning.

PRAISE

Verbal recognition of an appropriate behavior, which motivates your child to use that behavior on a regular basis.
Always direct praise at your child's behavior and not at your child. For example, say, "Nice building with the blocks," not "Good boy for building the block tower." When you say the latter, you are doing something you don't want to do – connecting a child's worth to his behavior. You don't want to teach a child that as long as he's behaving appropriately, he's a good person.

We believe that all children are inherently good. Their behavior may need to change – but they are still the same wonderful people. Praising the appropriate thing your child is doing reminds him of your expectations and reinforces your model of good behavior. Praise motivates your child to continue behaving appropriately.

QUIET GAME

A fun game to play with your child at bedtime to discourage her from talking, asking questions, and generally trying to keep you at her side so she can put off going to sleep.
To begin the game, simply say, "Let's play the quiet game. See how long you can stay quiet. The game starts now." Then wait outside the door for 60 seconds before whispering "You are being so quiet. I know you will win the quiet game." After two more minutes,

whisper, "You are being so quiet." By then, your child will be either asleep or so drowsy she will want to go to sleep.

You can also play a version of the quiet game with your child when you want her to be quiet in places such as libraries, religious services, hospitals, or anyplace where good manners require quiet. In this version, simply say, "We're playing the quiet game now. Let's see how long you can be quiet." Whisper praises to your child about how quiet she is being during this time to encourage her to practice these good manners.

REPRIMAND

A short statement that includes the following directions:

1. A command to stop the behavior
2. A reason to stop the behavior
3. A new behavior that replaces the old one

For example, you might say to your child, "Stop hitting. Hitting hurts people. Ask your friend nicely to give you the ball."

RULE

A rule can be defined in several ways, including as follows:

1. A predetermined behavioral expectation
2. A boundary that draws the line between inappropriate and appropriate behavior
3. An internal structure that guides appropriate behavior

Establishing and enforcing rules is an effective problem-solving technique. Children will behave more appropriately and feel more confident when their world has clear boundaries and when they can anticipate the consequences of their behavior. A rule becomes an internal structure that acts as guidance for your child in your absence.

Also, telling your child "The rule is X," will help him understand that following rules is important. And following rules is a skill you want him to learn now and practice throughout his life.

A rule includes a stated outcome and consequences. For example, one of your rules might be "We put our dirty clothes in the basket when we take them off. This helps us keep our house neat." To help your child remember the rule, use praise. For example, say, "Thank you for remembering the clothes-in-the-basket rule." If your child does not remember the rule, he is telling you that you need to spend more time telling him the rule so he can practice it.

SELF-TALK

What you say to yourself that can either help you resolve a situation (positive self-talk) or make it worse (negative self-talk)
When you can calm yourself in times of stress by using positive self-talk, you will be more likely to follow through with reasonable and responsible actions. Basic to positive self-talk is the ability to separate who you are from your behavior by saying for example "I'm a good person even if I make mistakes as a parent." This kind of positive self-talk helps you set yourself up for success.

Positive self-talk avoids exaggerations, such as the words *always* and *never.*

Never say, for example, "My daughter ALWAYS hits her brother," or "He NEVER listens to me." *Always* and *never* mean forever and ever, which makes this self-talk not true. On the other hand, positive self-talk in this case would be, "My daughter sometimes hits her brother, and I can deal with that."

Using positive self-talk also helps you avoid blowing events out of proportion by making them disasters and telling yourself that you can't stand it. For example, saying "I can't stand it when my child whines!" is an exaggeration because not only have you withstood your child's whining, but you can continue to tolerate it. When you tell yourself that you can't stand it, your level of tolerance for the whining is greatly diminished, which can lead to a damaging reaction to your child. Positive self-talk in this case would be "This whining will not kill me, and I can deal with it even though I don't like it." When you say this, not only will you be able to tolerate the whining longer, but you will also be more likely to plan effective ways of responding to your child's behavior.

Positive self-talk will lead you to be calm with a low level of stress, whereas negative self-talk leads to powerful negative emotions, such as anger, frustration, anxiety, and fear – all of which cause a stress reaction in your brain and block your ability to solve problems. Positive self-talk also avoids using the exaggerating words *must* and *should,* which lead to demands that you cannot meet, such as "I *should* be a better parent." When you say, "I'd like to be a better parent," you reduce the mandate and make it a desire, which is a much more reasonable and reachable goal.

Sometimes, parents sabotage themselves with self-talk that encourages them to follow the crowd. For example, if your child's friend's parents let your child use a bed as a trampoline, you may feel pressured to do the same by telling yourself that you would be a bad parent if you didn't let him do that and that it would be awful to not be in the "good-parent-club." So you let your bed become a trampoline so that you can follow the crowd. This peer-pressure self-talk can also be harmless, as in when you buy a certain kind of peanut butter because other parents buy it. But follow-the-crowd self-talk can be dangerous if it leads you to yell at or spank your child because the other moms and dads do.

To encourage your child to learn positive self-talk, model your own positive self-talk by talking aloud when you are resolving difficult events. For example, if your child spills his milk and your self-talk automatically goes to "This is awful! What a disaster," shift to positive self-talk and say aloud, "No big deal. Let's get the sponge and clean it up." Keeping your self-talk calm and constructive as a model will help your child avoid the bad habit of exaggerating events as awful and terrible instead of treating them realistically as tolerable and fixable.

Section Five

Let's Do It!

Solving the 43 Most Common Childhood Behavior Problems

"There are only two lasting bequests
we can hope to give our children.
One of them is roots, the other, wings."
– Johann Wolfgang von Goethe

We have organized the solution to each of the behavioral problems listed in this section into four parts, one of which we have subdivided to help you clearly understand what to do and what not to do. Here's a brief overview of each part:

Defining the Problem: Each solution begins with a brief discussion of why the behavioral problem in question is so common and normal for young children and why children exhibit it.

Preventing the Problem: The second part of each solution gives concrete suggestions about how to organize your life and your child's life to reduce the frequency and duration of the behavioral problem.

Solving the Problem: The third part of each solution gives practical directions to help you solve the behavioral problem. We present these directions in the clearest form possible: *What to Do* and *What Not to Do.*

What to Do: To solve the problem most effectively, think of each *What to Do* suggestion as a remedy for a certain behavior that you see as a problem. The guiding principle for changing children's behavior is "Try the simplest strategy first." This usually means showing your child what to do and encouraging him to do it. If that doesn't work, try the next-easiest strategy and proceed from there until you find the *What to Do* suggestion that works.

What Not to Do: It's equally important to know what *not* to do for each behavior that you think of as a problem. So pay special attention to the *What Not to Do* suggestions listed. These will help you prevent certain behavioral problems from recurring, becoming worse, or creating another problem.

Bear in mind that because parents and children are individuals, certain words and actions as applied in specific situations will feel more natural to some people than to others. So feel free to change a word or two of our suggested language if the exact language that we provide doesn't flow comfortably from your mouth. Young children are acutely aware of and sensitive to the feelings and subtle reactions of their parents and parenting team members, so you need to make what you say and do believable to your children. That will make them more readily accept your discipline.

The solutions in this book are designed to show your child the kind of respect you would give others in your home. Your children learn to be respectful by being treated respectfully, so treat your child as if he were a guest in your house. This does not mean your child shouldn't follow the rules; it means you should encourage him in a kind and respectful way to follow the rules.

Case History: The fourth and last part of each solution includes a case history that illustrates how a fictionalized family has used the *What to Do* and *What Not to Do* strategies to solve that specific behavioral problem.

Aggressive Behavior and Bullying

DEFINING THE PROBLEM

When young children hurl toys, teasing words, or their bodies at the nearest targets out of frustration, anger, or the need to dominate another child or an adult, we often don't describe such behavior with the term *bullying.* But that's what it is. Bullying is defined as treating a person in an overbearing or intimidating manner or being aggressive by being intimidating, frightening, terrorizing, or domineering. Examples of bullying include hitting, biting, scratching, pinching, throwing, name-calling, and teasing.

Just as spanking a child is a bullying behavior that you may find "works" in the short term – the spanked child might do what you want her to do, for example, out of fear – children's aggressive, bullying behavior may help them get their way in the short term as well. But bullying is not a long-term solution for them to use when they are angry or frustrated, or to get what they want.

So as a caring, protective adult, it's important to teach children from early on how this behavior hurts other people and is therefore not acceptable. Make it your number-one priority to prevent your child from using aggressive behavior and bullying. Do this by teaching her to regulate her emotions when she is upset and wants to exercise her power to get what she wants.

Note: If your child's aggressive, bullying behavior is a regular feature of her daily play and is disruptive to friends, family, and yourself, seek professional help to find out what may be causing this behavior. Also note that children who are spanked more than twice a month at age three are *twice as likely* to be aggressive by age five, so avoid spanking to avoid bullying.

PREVENTING THE PROBLEM

Use Understanding and Empathy

You cannot have empathy for others and be a bully at the same time. When your child uses aggression, try to put yourself in her position so that you can understand her motivation. Then help her understand what happens to others when she is aggressive. Tell her such things as "I understand you were frustrated, but how do you think James felt when you threw that truck at him?"

Talking about feelings and how hurtful words can be will help your child refocus on the impact her words have on others. Talk about how hurt you felt when someone said something mean to you.

Closely Supervise Your Child's Play

To prevent your child from learning aggressive behavior from her peers, monitor how she and her friends interact with each other and how they care for their toys. Don't let aggressive behavior cause injury or damage. Also respond to your child's friends' aggressive behavior as you would to your own child's.

Keep Yourself Under Control

Using aggression – such as spanking, yelling, slapping, or threatening – when you are angry or upset with your child or anyone else only teaches that aggression is okay. Remember that a harmful, toxic stress response results when your child feels threatened by *your* aggressive reaction to her aggressive behavior! Showing self-control when your child seems out of control will not only model positive behavior for your child, but it will also help you teach her what to do besides hurt other people when she is upset.

Avoid Aggressive or Violent Electronic Media

A diet of violent screen time can cause your child to imitate what she sees on the screen without realizing that aggressive actions in real life actually *do* hurt people. Watching violent media also provokes a toxic stress response in children, and that is a dangerous brain changer. (See Section Two, page 9)

SOLVING THE PROBLEM

What to Do

Teach Your Child What Words and Names Are Appropriate and Inappropriate to Use

Make sure you've educated your child about using hurtful words and names before expecting her to know what they are. For example, even though she may hear her friends at preschool, at daycare, or on TV calling someone stupid, your rule is that calling people hurtful names like "stupid" or telling them to shut up is not acceptable.

Ask for an Apology

Asking your child to apologize for calling a person names guides her to feel empathy for the person she offended. Use Grandma's Rule by saying "When you have told your friend how sorry you are for calling him a name, then you may go back to your play."

Remove Your Child from the Situation

When your child is acting aggressively, it's important to stop her immediately and remove her from the situation where she is displaying that behavior. Taking a short calm time will reduce the anger that drove the aggression and will allow you to calmly discuss the issue with her. Ask your child to name the things she can do besides hit when she's feeling upset. She may need some prompting, so you can tell her to ask an adult for help in that situation or to tell the other children "I'm not playing anymore," and simply leave the playgroup. Ask her to practice these lines and this action five times until she's familiar with the words and actions. This translates a thought into action.

Talk with Your Child About What to Do When She's Upset, Instead of Acting Aggressively

Tame your child's aggressive behavior by first explaining that any kind of aggression – pinching, hitting, biting, throwing, pushing, or teasing – is wrong. Then show and tell (even your under one year-old who hits you while you're diapering her) the right kind of behavior that you want her to exhibit when she is upset. Also, remember that boys are more likely to behave aggressively, as we noted in Understand the Difference Between Boys and Girls, see page 21.

If your child is not yet able to verbally solve problems with you, it is critical that you observe her closely and redirect her to another kind of play *before* her anger escalates to aggression.

Compliment Getting Along with Others

To explain what you mean by getting along with others, tell your child you appreciate her behavior when she shares, takes turns, asks for help, and so on. For example, say, "Good sharing with your friends, sweetheart." Always be specific about what you are praising. The more you praise your child's behavior, the more that behavior will be repeated.

Use Reprimands

Reprimanding your child helps her understand which of her behaviors you disapprove of and why. It also shows that you respect your child's ability to understand your reasons for disapproving of her behavior. The three parts of an effective reprimand for hitting include the following:

1. Tell your child to stop. ("Stop hitting!")
2. Explain why you disapprove. ("Hitting hurts people!").
3. Suggest an acceptable alternative to hitting. ("When you feel angry, just leave the group.")

Forget the Incident When It's Over

Reminding your child of her previous aggressions doesn't teach her acceptable behavior. On the contrary, it reminds her of how she could be aggressive again.

What Not to Do

Watch Your Name-Calling and Labeling

Because being called names is so irritating, it's easy to shout back at your child with the same hurtful words she says to you. Saying something like "You dummy! You should know better than to call people names," gives your young child permission to use the names you use. Instead, channel your anger into an explanation of how and why you feel upset. Your child will learn when you find her words unacceptable and how you'd like her to behave when she feels like name-calling.

Don't Punish for Name-Calling

If you punish your child for name-calling, she'll only learn to avoid name-calling when you're within earshot. Instead of learning that name-calling is wrong, she'll learn that she needs to avoid getting caught. Punished behavior does not go away; it just goes out of sight.

Don't Model Aggression and Name-Calling

Cursing at a driver who cut you off will tell your child that it's okay to call people names when she's angry. To reduce your own anger and as a model of self-regulation for your child, try saying "Cutting me off while I was driving was dangerous. I hope that other driver doesn't have an accident before she gets where she is going."

Don't Use Aggression to Stop Aggression

Slapping or spanking your child only gives her permission to hit others in similar circumstances, and hitting her causes a toxic stress response that can lead to behavior issues and cognitive and health problems for her. (See Section Three, page 25)

CASE HISTORY: MIKE THE HITTER

At three years old, Mike Morgan became known as the neighborhood hitter. He'd had lots of practice on his two older brothers, who had bullied him by teasing him mercilessly. Vivian Morgan threatened her youngest child in order to stop his aggressiveness, saying "If you don't stop hitting people, Mikey, I'm going to spank you." But she knew she couldn't back up her threat. The very idea of hitting a child just made her cringe, and hitting her child to stop him from hitting didn't make sense to her!

However, Mikey's five and seven year-old brothers' bullying of him didn't seem to bother her. In fact, her family joked frequently about lots of things, and she considered the older boys' making fun of Mikey all in the spirit of not taking yourself too seriously. Besides, it would toughen Mikey up for the cold, cruel world he would have to enter someday – or so she reasoned.

But Mikey s dad didn't agree. "How do you think Mikey feels about being teased?" he asked one day. Though she didn't want to admit it, Vivian had never thought about this problem from Mikey's point of view – that he got back at his brothers by hitting because he couldn't match their verbal attacks. Vivian had often told him to use words instead, advising him to say, "I don't like to be teased." But it wasn't working. Using words just wasn't enough to stop his brothers from bullying him.

So she decided to teach all three boys that name-calling, hitting, teasing, and throwing things would not be tolerated. She believed that this was the only way to teach the older boys to model good behavior and to teach Mikey to make better choices about how to deal with his brothers. So the next time Mikey began attacking his brothers, after they called him "Little Oscar the Grouch," Vivian reprimanded Mikey first. She said, "Stop hitting, Mikey. Hitting hurts people. We don't hit people." But then she also reprimanded Mikey's brothers, saying "Stop teasing. We do not tease people. It hurts their feelings."

But the reprimands didn't stop the boys' verbal and physical attacks. So Vivian said, "I'm sorry you're still hitting and teasing each other. I will take you to calm time!" She then directed the three boys to separate chairs and told them to think about what had happened and about ways in which they could avoid having it happen again.

As Vivian became consistent in her discipline, and as she praised the boys when they got along nicely, they learned what to expect from fighting and from being friendly and treating each other nicely. Mikey began to hit less since he didn't have to tolerate his brothers' teasing, and the older boys became more empathetic as they learned that teasing was hurtful.

Bad Manners

DEFINING THE PROBLEM

Good manners are important social graces that establish a caring environment in which to work and play. In fact, good manners are the basic social rules people must follow to avoid offending each other, intentionally or unintentionally. In short, using good manners helps people feel comfortable and at ease with each other.

You may have found that teaching good manners to your young child is not an easy task, for a variety of reasons. First of all, young children are very egocentric. They generally think only of their own needs and not the needs of others. But even though good manners may not seem important to your child in his me-first mind, teaching your child good manners is part of helping him understand how others feel and how his behavior impacts others.

So how can you teach your young child to understand the need to say, "Excuse me," when he interrupts? How can you teach him to say please and thank you? Do it by carefully teaching him in a consistently caring and respectful way, using the strategies below.

PREVENTING THE PROBLEM

Start Early

Even before your child can say the words *please* and *thank you,* set the stage by using these words yourself. When changing a diaper, giving a bath, and feeding your little one, describe your behaviors by using good manners. Say, "Thank you for playing so nicely in the tub, Johnny!" Your child is listening!

SOLVING THE PROBLEM

What to Do

Set Rules for Manners
Keeping it simple, begin manners training by outlining a few rules, such as when to say please and thank you.

Model Good Manners
It is also good to point out your own good manners when you use them. You can say, "Please put the book on the table. See, I used the word *please* because that's the rule, and it's a polite way to ask someone to do something. That means I'm using good manners."

Praise Good Manners
When your child follows a manners rule, tell him how nice it sounds when he says please and thank you. Also tell him that using good manners makes others feel respected. Praise his good table manners by saying such things as "You are using your spoon so nicely," or "Thank you for chewing with your mouth closed."

Practice Manners

Play is life practice for children, so having a pretend tea party allows you to introduce good table manners and model them through play. Then you can transfer those same manners to the dinner table.

Correct Bad Manners

When your child forgets the manners rule, say, "Remember the rule: we eat with our fork, not our hands," or, "Remember, we say thank you when someone does something nice for us."

What Not to Do

Don't Nag

Don't say, "How many times do I have to tell you to chew with your mouth closed?" Nagging offers no motivation for your child to follow your directions. Nagging only teaches a child to tune you out and to use nagging to motivate others. It doesn't teach him to value manners or show him how to use good manners.

Don't Belittle and Shame

Don't say, "You are eating like a pig," or, "Aren't you ashamed you didn't say thank you when Grandma gave you a treat?" Belittling and shaming a child doesn't teach him good manners. Trying to motivate a child by shaming him tells him that your love is conditional, which means that you only love him when he follows your rules.

Don't Make Dinner a Manners Battle

Rather than continually barking orders at your child to use good manners – saying "Sit up straight!" or "Use your fork!" or "Use your napkin!" – praise little bits of progress by saying "I like the way you picked up your fork. It's so nice to see you use a fork instead of your fingers to eat broccoli."

CASE HISTORY: MIA LEARNS MANNERS

At two and a half years of age, Mia was beginning to act like a real person; but she was very uncivilized, her parents Lillian and Thomas thought. They tried eating dinner with her by placing her in a booster seat so she could be at the table with the adults. But Mia would unbuckle her safety belt and climb onto the table to get more food for her plate. And then she'd stuff the food into her mouth until it was so full that Lillian and Thomas feared she would choke. They tried taping the buckle on Mia's booster seat safety belt so she couldn't unbuckle it; but then she only screamed. They tried bribing Mia with a sweet dessert, but when she didn't do as she was told, she screamed when they put the dessert away. Dinnertime was a war. Going out to eat was totally out of the question.

"Maybe we started teaching her manners too soon," Thomas suggested.

"Maybe, but she has learned so many new things. Surely she can learn simple manners," Lil replied.

Mia's parents decided to try again, but they thought a few practice sessions were in order. When Mia was in her booster seat, Lil stood behind her and guided Mia's spoon-filled hand from the dish to her mouth while Thomas praised the effort.

"Look at that," he said. "Mia is eating so nicely with her spoon."

After Mia began using her spoon correctly, Lillian and Thomas started praising her small bites and then showed her how to ask for more of something and say please. It took a while, but Mia began learning basic table manners and started receiving much praise for her efforts. Dinnertime became pleasant again.

Bathing and Diapering Battles

DEFINING THE PROBLEM

It's expected and even predicted that young children will find cleanup routines distasteful, so don't feel alone as you persevere with rinsing and soaking. Try to make the cleanup tasks less tedious by diverting your child's attention (for example, by singing songs and telling stories) and by praising any cooperation (even just handing you the soap).

If you are thinking that your child will be less resistant to bathing as he grows older, think again. Some children may not want to take time out of their playtime to do something as tedious as bathing themselves, so age may not make cleaning up less of a challenge.

Note: Distinguish between your child's reactions to products that physically irritate him (e.g., that burn his eyes) and his cries telling you that he just doesn't like to be messed with while he's playing in the tub. Most parents can tell the difference between distress cries and those that are motivated by anger, frustration, or the desire for attention. Distress cries don't change in tone or duration when parents or other distractions intrude. Other cries generally occur in short bursts interrupted by pauses during which the child listens for a reaction from parents or other parenting team members. If necessary, switch from products that physically irritate your child to those that are professionally recommended.

PREVENTING THE PROBLEM

Compromise on Cleanup Times and Places

Be flexible about cleanup routines, such as where you diaper your baby or toddler (for example, on the couch or standing up), when you wash his hair, or when he bathes. To avoid your child's fighting cleanup routines, fit them into his schedule as much as possible so he won't have to stop a favorite activity just to clean up.

Involve Your Child in the Process

Help your child play a part in the cleanup or diapering routine. Ask him to bring you things he can carry (according to his age, skill level, and ability to follow directions). Let him pick a favorite toy or towel, for example, to give him a feeling of control over the bathtime routine.

Prepare Your Child for the Cleanup Event

Give your child some warning before a bath, for example, to make the transition from playtime to bathtime less abrupt. Say, "When the timer rings, it will be time for the tub," or, "In a few minutes, we will change your diaper," or, "When we finish this book, it will be time for your bath."

Gather Materials Before Starting

If your child is too young to help you prepare, make sure you get things ready before beginning the cleanup. This helps avoid unnecessary delays and minimizes frustrations on both ends.

Develop a Positive Attitude

Your child will pick up on the dread in your voice if you announce bathtime like it's a prison sentence. If you sound worried or anxious, you're telling him it must be as horrible as he thought. Your attitude is contagious, so make it one that you want imitated.

Make the Bathtub an Ocean of Adventure

Lots of water toys and pouring cups and pitchers can make tub time more fun. Beware, however – if a young child has a cup in the bath, he might drink the bathwater!

SOLVING THE PROBLEM

WHAT TO DO

Remain Calm and Ignore the Noise

A calm mood is contagious when dealing with your upset child. So don't pay attention to the noise – just keep caring for and loving your child while you bathe him. He will learn that noise doesn't stop the process of getting clean, which is what he wants. Say to yourself, *I know my child needs to be diapered. If I don't pay attention to his noise, I'll get this done faster and more effectively.*

Have Fun in the Process

Distract your child by talking, playing, reciting nursery rhymes, or singing. Make it a monologue if your child is too young to participate verbally.

Encourage Your Child to Help and Shower Him with Praise

Ask your child to wash his own tummy, rub on the soap, or open the diaper (if time permits), to give him a feeling of controlling and participating in his personal hygiene. Even the slightest sign of cooperation is a signal for praise.

Also, slather on the words of encouragement. The more your child gets attention for acting as you'd prefer, the more he'll repeat the action to get your strokes. Say, "I really like how you put that shampoo on your hair," or, "That's great, the way you're sitting up in the tub," or, "Thanks for lying down so nicely while I diaper you."

Exercise Grandma's Rule

Let your child know that when he's done something you want him to do (like taking a bath), he can do something he wants to do (like read a story). Say, "When your bath is over, then we'll have a story," or, "When we're finished, then you can play with your blocks."

Persist in the Task at Hand

Despite the kicking, screaming, and yelling, be determined to finish the cleanup process. The more your child sees that his yelling isn't going to prevent you from washing away the dirt, the more he'll understand that you'll get the job done faster if he takes the path of least resistance.

Compliment Your Child when You're Done

Tell your child how delightful he looks and smells. Ask him to go look in the mirror. This will remind him of why he needs to have a bath or have his diaper changed. Learning to take pride in being clean will help him make cleanliness a priority.

What Not to Do

Don't Demand Cooperation

Just because you demand that your child get diapered doesn't mean he's going to lie still while you do it. Don't punish lack of cooperation. Acting rough and tough yourself only teaches him to be rough and tough, too.

Don't Make Cleanup Painful

Try to make cleanup as comfortable as possible for your child. Provide towels he can use to wipe his eyes, make the bathwater temperature just right, wrap him in a robe after you're done, and so on.

Don't Avoid Cleanup

Just because your child resists doesn't mean you should back down. Resistance to cleanup can be overcome by persistence, practice, and patience.

CASE HISTORY: OCEANS OF FUN

Carol and Phil Porter bathed and shampooed their two-year-old daughter, Lauren, just as they thought most parents they knew did. But they feared something was wrong with Lauren when she screamed and fought her way through these normal cleanup routines. The Porters never had experienced this problem with their other daughter, Elizabeth, and none of their friends had ever complained about it.

The Porters talked to their pediatrician, who assured them that the soaps, water, and towels were not harmful or irritating. Phil thought stricter discipline was needed, but they eventually agreed that the best approach was to make cleanup more appetizing to Lauren. The only water-related activity Lauren enjoyed was swimming in the Pacific Ocean during summer vacation, so the Porters decided to call bath-time Oceans of Fun.

That evening, they set the phone timer to sound when it was time to get in the "ocean." (Of course, they kept the phone FAR away from the water!) During trips to California, they had always set the phone timer to sound when they could go in the real ocean, because Lauren was always begging to get in the water. They hoped this technique would prove helpful at home in Minneapolis, too.

"When the timer sounds, it will be time to play Oceans of Fun," Carol told Lauren. "Let's finish this book while we're waiting." When the timer went off, Lauren and her mother gathered towels and soap, and Lauren excitedly asked questions about the new game. Lauren smiled with delight as her mom led her to the bathroom, where she found the bluest "ocean" she'd ever seen (the result of blue bubble bath) and jaunty boats cruising around a toy ship holding a container of soap (toys Carol bought to add to the experience).

Lauren jumped in without a push or an invitation and began playing with the ocean toys. Her mother started singing a song about a tugboat, and she gave Lauren a handful of shampoo to wash her own hair for the first time. The cleanup continued without yelling or screaming – and with just a little too much splashing. Carol began bathing Lauren in the ocean at least once a day, to give her opportunities to learn how to splash less, wash herself more carefully, and enjoy the experience.

Bedtime Battles

DEFINING THE PROBLEM

Active, energetic young children often do anything to avoid sleep. They turn bedtime or naptime into chase time, crying time, or finding-another-book-to-read time – all to postpone the dreaded going to bed. No matter what your child may think about the right time to go to sleep, stand firm with the time you have chosen. However, help your child gradually wind down, instead of requiring her to instantly turn off her motor.

Note: Since your child's need for sleep changes as she gets older, you may want to let her stay up later or shorten her naps as she grows. Children (even ones in the same family) require different amounts of sleep. Your two-year-old may not need the same amount of sleep her older brother did when he was two.

PREVENTING THE PROBLEM

Establish a Bedtime Routine

To end the day or begin a nap with a special feeling between you and your child, recite a poem or story as a regular part of the going-to-bed routine. Make bedtime special so it's something she can look forward to. Try reciting a phrase from a favorite book or having a talk about the day's events, even if it's a one-sided conversation. Routines are important because they let children predict what will happen next. You can make your routine longer or shorter as long as the events remain in the same order – for example: clothes off, bath, pajamas on, story, song, kiss, lights off.

Make Exercise a Daily Habit

Make sure your child gets plenty of exercise during the day, to help her body tell her mind that going to bed is a good idea.

Maintain a Fairly Regular Nap Schedule

Don't let your child put off napping until late afternoon or evening and then expect her to go to sleep at eight o'clock. Put her down for naps early enough in the day that she'll be tired again at bedtime.

Spend Time Together Before Bed

Play with your child before bedtime arrives, to prevent her from fighting bedtime just to get your attention. Make sure bedtime play is calm and quiet rather than noisy and hurried.

Keep Bedtime Consistent

Determine how much sleep your child needs by noticing how she acts when she has or hasn't taken a nap and when she has gone to bed at nine o'clock versus seven o'clock. Establish a consistent sleep schedule that meets her needs and adjust it as she gets older.

SOLVING THE PROBLEM

What to Do

Use a Phone Timer to Manage the Bedtime Routine

An hour before bedtime (or naptime), set your smartphone timer for five minutes and announce that the phone will tell your child when it's time to start getting ready for bed. This avoids surprises and allows her to anticipate the upcoming events.

When the phone timer sounds, say, "The phone says it's time to start getting ready for bed. Let's take a bath and get into our pajamas." Then reset the phone timer to about 15 minutes for the bath. When the timer rings, say, "The timer says that it's time to get out of the bathtub. Now let's see if we can beat the timer getting pajamas on." This gives you the opportunity to praise your child's efforts at getting herself through the basic bedtime routine.

Make Sure You Allow Enough Time for Her to Get the Job Done

When the routine is finished, reset the phone for the remainder of the hour you set aside and announce, "You beat the phone timer. Now you get to stay up and play until the phone sounds again and tells us that it's time to get into bed. Now, let's set the phone for brushing our teeth, getting a drink, and going potty (if she's old enough)." The phone timer routine helps you and your child make a game, instead of a struggle, out of bedtime.

Follow the Same Rituals Regardless of Time

Even if bedtime has been delayed for some reason, go through the same rituals to help your child learn what's expected of her when it comes to going to bed. Don't point out how late she's stayed up. Quicken the pace by helping her get her pajamas on and get a drink and setting the timer for shorter intervals. But don't omit any steps since children thrive on routine.

Maintain the Same Order of Events

Since young children find comfort in consistency, have your child bathe, brush her teeth, and put on her pajamas in the same order every night. Ask her to name the next step in the routine. This will help to make a game out of getting ready for bed and will help her feel as if she's calling the shots.

Offer Benefits for Going to Bed

Teach your child that going to bed on time is worthwhile. Say, "Because you got into bed on time, I'll read you an extra story."

What Not to Do

Don't Let Your Child Control Bedtime

Stick with your chosen bedtime despite your child's resistance. Remember that you know why your child doesn't want to go to bed – and why she should. Say to yourself, "She's only crying because she doesn't want to end her playtime, but I know she'll play happier later if she sleeps now."

Don't Threaten

Threatening your child to get her into bed can cause nightmares and fears, not to mention making you feel upset. Punishing a child doesn't teach her appropriate behavior. Instead, focus on using your phone timer as a neutral authority to determine when bedtime arrives.

Don't Be a Historian

Saying "Because you didn't go to bed on time last night, you don't get to play on the computer this morning," doesn't teach your child how to get into bed on time. Focus on the future instead of the past.

CASE HISTORY: BEDTIME AT BEN'S

Evenings at the Shores' house meant one thing: a tearful battle of wills at bedtime between three-year-old Benjamin and his father, Andrew.

"I'm not tired! I don't want to go to bed! I want to stay up!" Ben would plead each night as his angry father dragged him to bed.

"I know you don't want to go to bed," Andrew would reply, "but you will do what I say, and I say it's bedtime!" Forcing Ben to go to bed upset Andrew as much as it did Ben. Even though Andrew believed he should be the boss, he knew there had to be a way to avoid the battles and Ben's crying himself to sleep.

So the next night, Andrew decided to control himself and let something else – his smartphone timer – control bedtime. An hour before Ben's bedtime, Andrew set his timer for five minutes. "It's time to start getting ready for bed," Andrew explained to his curious son. "If you get yourself ready for bed before the phone sounds, we'll set the phone again and you can stay up and play until it sounds."

Ben raced around and got ready for bed before the phone sounded. As promised, Andrew reset his phone, read Ben his favorite animal tales, and sang some new sleepytime songs until the phone sounded again almost an hour later.

"It's time for bed, right?" Ben announced, acting delighted to have this game all figured out.

"That's right! I'm so proud of you for remembering the new rule," his dad replied.

As the two journeyed up to bed, Andrew once again told Ben how proud he was of Ben's getting himself ready for bed. Using the phone to control bedtime routines helped them enjoy a painless evening for the first time in months. And after several weeks of following this routine, going to bed still wasn't something to look forward to, but it was a far cry from the old struggles between Ben and his dad.

Car Seat Resistance

DEFINING THE PROBLEM

Car seats and seat belts are the enemies of millions of freedom-loving young children – adventurous spirits who don't understand why they must be strapped down. But they can understand the rule that the car doesn't move until they're strapped into their car seats or their belts are on. So ensure your own and your child's safety every time she gets into a car by enforcing the belts-on rule. The seat belt habit will become second nature to your child – a passenger today and a driver tomorrow – if you're not wishy-washy about this life-or-death rule.

And for your own safety, a wild child bouncing around unrestrained in the car is a dangerous distraction. Also, every state now requires that infants and children be buckled up when riding in a motor vehicle. Approved car seats and seat belts have weight and age specifications to make car travel as safe as possible for your child. Finally, the leading cause of death for American children is trauma from automobile accidents. This trauma can be prevented by making sure children are properly restrained.

Never compromise the rule about being buckled up or you may be compromising your child's life.

For more information and recommendations on car seats, check the American Academy of Pediatrics (AAP) website at https://www.aap.org/en-us/advocacy-and-policy/state-advocacy/documents/child_passenger_safety_slr.pdf.

PREVENTING THE PROBLEM

Give Your Child Room to Breathe

Make sure she has room to move her hands and legs and still be safely buckled up.

Make a Rule That the Car Will Not Move Unless Everyone Is Buckled Up

If you enforce this rule from the beginning, your child will become accustomed to the idea of sitting in a car seat and eventually wearing a seat belt.

Make Your Child Proud to Be Safe

Tell your child why she's graduating to a booster seat or using only a seat belt. This will make her proud of being strapped in. For example, say, "You're getting to be so grown-up. Here's your new safety seat for the car!"

Conduct a Training Program

Let your child know how you expect her to act in a car. Take short drives around the neighborhood with one parent or friend driving and the other praising your child for sitting nicely in her car seat. Say, "You're sitting in your car seat so nicely today."

SOLVING THE PROBLEM

What to Do

Buckle Yourself Up

Make sure to wear your seat belt and point out how your child is wearing one, too, to help her understand that she's not alone in her temporary confinement. If you don't wear a seat belt, your child will not understand why she has to.

Praise Staying in the Seat Belt

If you ignore your child while she's riding nicely, she may look for ways to get your attention, including trying to get out of her car seat or seat belt. Keep your child out of trouble in the car by talking to her and playing word games, as well as by praising how nicely she's sitting.

Be Consistent

Stop the car as quickly and safely as possible every time your child gets out of her car seat or seat belt. This will teach her that the rule will be enforced. Say, "The car will move again only when you're back in your car seat (or seat belt) so you will be safe."

Divert Your Child's Attention

Try activities such as number games, word games, Peek-a-Boo, singing songs, and so on. This will prevent your child from trying to get out of her seat because she needs something to do. Conversation with you is much more valuable to her than what she can watch on TV, so avoid entertaining her only with the in-car TV.

What Not to Do

Don't Complain About Having to Wear a Seat Belt

Casually telling your spouse or friend that you hate wearing a seat belt gives your child a reason to resist her belt, too.

Don't Pay Attention to Your Child's Yelling about Being Buckled In, Unless She Unfastens Her Seat Belt or Gets Out of Her Car Seat

Not giving attention to your child's crying or whining while she's belted in helps her see that there's no benefit in protesting the seat belt rule. Say to yourself, "I know my child is safer in her car seat and will only fight it temporarily. Her safety is my responsibility, and I am fulfilling that responsibility by enforcing the seat belt rule."

Don't Use Threats or Fear

Telling your child about the grave dangers of being out of her car seat won't teach her how to stay in it. Threatening to take away toys or privileges later in the day won't teach her to follow the rules, either.

Don't Spank!

Spanking or threatening to spank her for getting out of her car seat will only hurt you both and won't teach your child how to stay buckled up. You can't be a caring adult and use violence or threats of violence at the same time.

CASE HISTORY: UNBUCKLED JACOB

Stephan Brenner loved to take his four-year-old son, Jacob, on errands with him – until his son figured out how to get his father's undivided attention by unbuckling his seat belt and jumping around in the backseat. "Don't you ever undo that belt again, young man!" Stephan ordered when he saw that his son had gotten free. But simply demanding that Jacob stay put didn't solve the problem, so Stephan decided that harsher, more threatening punishment was necessary. Though he had not spanked his son before, he threatened to give him a swift swat on his bottom whenever he found him roaming unbuckled in the backseat.

However, to carry out the threat, Stephan had to stop the car whenever Jacob got out of his seat. And every time Stephan stopped the car, Jacob would scramble back into his seat and fasten his belt to avoid being walloped. So Stephan decided that instead of threatening Jacob, he would stop the car and refuse to continue until Jacob's belt was buckled.

Stephan tried this new method the next time they were on their way to the park. When Jacob unbuckled himself, Stephan stopped the car, saying "We can go to the park when you're back in your seat and buckled up. It's not safe for you to be unbuckled." Stephan crossed his fingers, hoping that Jacob would get back in his seat since Stephan knew Jacob was eager to get to the park. Jacob cooperated, but a few miles from home, Jacob unbuckled himself again and Stephan stopped the car again. He didn't spank his son; he simply repeated the rule: "The car will move again when you're back in your car seat." Jacob returned to his seat and calmly buckled himself in. Stephan told him "Thanks for getting back in your seat," and they drove home without incident.

That didn't end the problem, however. The next time Jacob released himself, Stephan was so angry he was tempted to yell and scream again. But he stuck to his new method. He also began to include Jacob in conversations and praise his safe behavior. After a while, Stephan was once again enjoying his outings with his son, assured that the two of them were traveling safely.

Car Travel Conflicts

DEFINING THE PROBLEM

A family road trip – be it a brief ride across town, several hours' driving to Grandma's, or a two-day vacation – can be fun, an ordeal, or lots of both! For many adults, taking a road trip offers a change of pace, scenery, and routine when cares of home are abandoned for the free and easy life of the open road. For many young children, however, a road trip is anything but fun, even with the car's built-in TV. Besides experiencing the confinement of a car seat, young ones will miss the sense of security offered by familiar toys, beds, toilets, and foods. The comforts of home are often absent when you're traveling, so teach your child how to cope with change and how to enjoy new experiences – two tasks made easier if you have a happy, interested pupil who feels secure in her new surroundings. (See Change Resistance, page 80) Also remember that children who are not buckled in safely will create dangerous distractions for the driver. For more information on car seat safety, see Car Seat Resistance, page 69.

PREVENTING THE PROBLEM

Check the Car Seat or Seat Restraints Before Traveling

The safety measures you take before leaving will determine how relaxed you are with your children when you finally depart. Don't wait until the last minute to find out that you must delay your trip because you lack an essential item: the safety seat.

Make Car Rules

Institute the rule that the car moves only when everyone is buckled in. Say, "I'm sorry your belt is not buckled. The car can't move until you're safely buckled in." Be prepared to wait until the passengers comply with your rule before you go.

Praise Good Car Behavior

As you and your child travel to and from school or run errands together, remember to praise his proper sitting in the car seat or using seat belts. This will show your child that staying in his car seat and being properly secured produces rewards.

Provide Appropriate Materials for Entertainment

Make sure you pack toys that are harmless to clothing and upholstery. Crayons are okay, but felt-tip pens are discouraged because they may permanently mark clothing and upholstery. Have age-appropriate materials for hand-held screens or the television DVD player.

Familiarize Your Child with Your Travel Plans

Discuss your travel plans with your child so she'll know how long you'll be gone, what will happen to her room while you're away, and when you'll return. Show her maps and photos of your destination. Talk to her about the people, scenery, and events you'll experience. Share personal stories and souvenirs from previous visits to the destination. If your child is anxious about going to an unknown place, compare the destination to one she's familiar with.

Personally Involve Your Child Traveler

Allow your child to participate in the preparation and execution of the trip. Enlist his help in packing his clothing, selecting car toys and media, and picking healthy drinks and snacks.

Establish Rules of Conduct for Traveling

Before you leave, explain to your child any special rules of the road. For example, you might establish a noise rule, an exploring rule, a pool rule, and a restaurant rule for stops along the way.

SOLVING THE PROBLEM

WHAT TO DO

Praise Good Behavior

Frequently praise good behavior and provide rewards for staying in car seats. For example, say, "I like the way you're looking at all the trees and houses. It's really a pretty day. We can get out soon and play in a playground because you've been sitting in your car seat so nicely."

Stop the Car If Your Child Gets out of Her Car Seat or Unbuckles Her Seat Belt

Make sure your child realizes that your car seat rule will be strictly enforced and that the consequences will be the same every time the rule is violated.

Play Car Games

Count objects, recognize colors, look for animals, and so on to keep your child entertained. Make a list of fun things to do before you leave home. Switch games as needed to maintain your child's (and your) interest.

Make Frequent Rest Stops

Your restless young child is usually happiest when he's mobile. Restraining him for hours in a car does not suit his adventurous spirit. Give him time to let off steam in a roadside park or rest stop or you'll find him rebelling when you least expect it.

Monitor Snacks on Long Trips

Highly sugared or carbonated foods or beverages may not only increase a child's activity level, but they may also increase the chance of your child's becoming carsick. Stick to protein snacks or lightly salted ones to keep her healthy and happy.

Use Grandma's Rule

Let your child know that good behavior on trips brings rewards. For example, if your child has been whining about getting a drink, say, "When you've sat in your seat and talked with us without whining, then we'll stop and get something to drink."

What Not to Do

Don't Let Young Children Sit in the Front Seat

No matter how much they fuss and beg to sit next to Mommy or Daddy in the front seat, young children should never be allowed to sit there, even on the shortest of trips. The safest place for young children is buckled safely in a car seat or booster seat in the back.

Don't Make Promises You May Not Fulfill

Don't be too specific about what your child will see on your travels, because he might hold you to it. For example, if you say you'll see a bear in Yellowstone Park and you don't, you might hear him whining as you leave "But you promised I'd see a bear."

Don't Rely Solely on In-Car Media for Entertainment

Even children who love TV and video games will eventually tire of them. That is why word games, puzzles, books, crayons, and other forms of entertainment are needed even on short trips.

CASE HISTORY: CAR WARS

Michael and Andrea Sterling wanted to take their children on a vacation that was just like the vacations they had each enjoyed when they were young. But even short trips in the car with three-year-old Zoe and six-year-old Zachary were more like punishment than a Sunday drive. The backseat of the car was a war zone, with the children's incessant screaming frequently leading Michael and Andrea to issue threats of spankings. But the threats didn't seem to help. The Sterlings, who often felt just as angry after making the threats as they did before, felt nearly hopeless about finding a solution to their car travel problems. Even getting a new car with a built-in TV didn't help because the children began to fight over what to watch.

Eventually, they decided to develop new rules for car trips. They found some toys that their kids could play with unsupervised, and they explained the new rules for car trips. "Kids," they began, "when we go to school in the morning, we want you to talk with us nicely all the way there. When you do that, you can each pick out your favorite kind of juice when we get home." They then applied and tested those rules not just on trips to school but on trips to daycare, the grocery store, the park, and friends' homes.

Initially, the kids followed the rules and the Sterlings praised them for it. "Thanks for being so cooperative with each other," they said. But the plan hit a roadblock when the kids returned to fighting about what they wanted to watch on TV in the car. However, it only took two more tests for the children to behave kindly toward each other and follow the car rules during the entire time in the car. They received praise for their efforts, and they were rewarded for their good behavior.

Two weeks later, the Sterling family began its two-hour trek to Grandma's, the longest trip in the car since the practice sessions had begun. The children knew what was expected of them and what rewards were available along the way and at their destination. Between short intervals of viewing TV, they played games and took turns picking shows and new games. The previous ordeal of a car ride soon became a pleasant experience for all!

Change Resistance

DEFINING THE PROBLEM

"No! Mommy do it!" your son shrieks as your husband tries to give him a bath, a job he says is Mommy's. Change can be hard for everybody, but it's particularly difficult for young children. It's even more trying for children born with a temperament that makes them want everything to be routine and predictable, causing them to want to have control over everything in their world.

Little ones haven't had much experience adjusting to change. So when you ask your little boy to get ready to leave when he's immersed in playing with a friend on a play date, or if you tell him the two of you are going to an unfamiliar place, he's likely to have a meltdown. Finding security in predictable sameness is common in young children, but sometimes the need for security borders on absolute inflexibility. So use the strategies below to help reticent children learn how to adapt to change.

PREVENTING THE PROBLEM

Teach Decision-Making Skills

Your child wants to feel that he's the master of his own fate, so allow him to make simple decisions. Choosing between two cereals, two pairs of socks, and two games to play gives him a sense of control over his world.

Respect Your Child's Individuality

You may have made friends with change long ago, but your child might have a more difficult time because his temperament might be different from yours. Understand that each child has a unique temperament, even within the same family. Avoid saying "Don't be like that!" when your child's inflexible feathers are ruffled. Instead, say, "I know it's hard for you to change babysitters. But you can handle it. It'll be okay."

SOLVING THE PROBLEM

What to Do

Build Resilience

Resilient children look at change as a challenge to be overcome. On the other hand, inflexible children resist change as much as possible. But telling your child he *gets to* do something rather than *has to* do it will transform his feelings of fear and loss of control into feelings of excitement. Help him build this framework for change by saying, "You get to have a new babysitter tonight. She's going to be lots of fun. Isn't it exciting getting to know someone new?"

Teach Your Child the Self-Talk to Handle Change by Modeling It Yourself

Children who are shown how to deal with change are more prepared to meet the challenge. Say, "My new shirt is very nice. Not getting to wear my old blue one is no big deal. I will feel so good wearing my new yellow shirt today."

Set Goals for Accepting Change

Children feel more in control of their destiny if they have ample time to think about and prepare themselves for change. You can help your child accept change more readily by having him set goals for handling change. For example, say, "We're going to the zoo with your class tomorrow. It'll be fun. Let's set a goal of having a good time at the zoo." Then periodically remind him of the goal and have him repeat it to you. Ask him "What's your goal about going to the zoo?" When he says, "I'm going to the zoo to have fun," say, "That's right, you're going to the zoo to have a good time."

Teach Problem Solving

When children are confronted with change and don't know what to do, giving them limited choices helps them see their options. Say, "I know you don't want to move into the big bed. Let's think about what we can do to make it easier. Maybe you could take your teddy bear into the big bed with you and he'll keep you company while you're there."

What Not to Do

Don't Meet Resistance with Anger

Children who are upset by change need lots of support and empathy to reduce their anxiety. Getting angry with your child for being inflexible only increases his sense of helplessness and doesn't help him learn to accept change.

CASE HISTORY: THE CUP-AND-BOWL CAPER

Julia Bardwell was only two and a half years old, but she had shown from very early on that she didn't like change. She rigidly resisted any new event that came into her young life. Her parents, Dena and Jim, knew better than to go against her wishes. If it wasn't a fight over using the blue cup instead of the yellow one at breakfast, it was a war over wearing something other than her green shorts and pink T-shirt. When confronted with change, Julia would first resist, then scream, and then finally melt into an inconsolable, tearful tirade.

Dena and Jim wanted to help Julia become more flexible and resilient. Jim knew that setting goals at work helped him stay focused and not get distracted by his anxiety over getting everything done. He thought that Julia might be able to see beyond her fear of change if she had a goal to think about. Dena and Jim decided that Julia's first goal would focus on her steadfast refusal to use different dishes at breakfast. Once she learned to be more flexible by using different dishes, she might be able to be less rigid in dealing with other changes. So they began by talking to Julia about getting a new cup-and-bowl set for breakfast, one they let her pick out herself.

That night, Dena said, "Julia, let's set a goal for tomorrow morning. I think it would be a good idea for your goal to be to have fun using your new cup and bowl when you have breakfast." Julia looked at her mother and nodded, but Dena wasn't sure the idea of a goal had sunk in. A few minutes later, Dena said, "Julia, remember your goal for tomorrow morning? You're going to have fun using your new cup and bowl."

This time, Julia answered, "Yeah, I 'member."

The Bardwells repeated this reminder several more times that evening. They even made an occasional trip to the kitchen to look at the cup and bowl sitting all shiny and new on the counter.

At breakfast the next morning, Julia eagerly headed for the table, saying "Where's my new cup and bowl?"

Dena and Jim knew they were on to something. They could help Julia accept change by helping her look forward to it. After a few days with the new cup and bowl, Dena and Jim said, "Julia, let's use the old blue cup and bowl at breakfast tomorrow."

"No!" Julia cried. "The new cup and bowl! I want the new cup and bowl!"

Dena and Jim didn't say anything about her digging in her heels like they had in the past. Instead, they decided to help her set a new goal. That evening, Dena said, "Julia, let's set a new goal for breakfast tomorrow. I'd like your new goal to be using the old blue cup and bowl." Later that evening, Dena said, "Julia, what's the new goal for breakfast tomorrow?"

Julia thought for a minute and said, "The blue cup and bowl?"

"That's right," Dena said. "We're going to use the blue ones tomorrow. I'm glad you remembered the new goal."

Although Dena and Jim weren't sure this little exercise would pay off, they were delighted when Julia started treating it like a game and actually looked forward to the new goal for the day. They knew that Julia could ease into change as long as she was prepared for it. They now had a plan that made the whole family happy. Their perseverance had paid off.

Climbing on Anything and Everything

DEFINING THE PROBLEM

Some children, especially boys, can't resist climbing on anything that looks climb-able – even if it isn't. These children will climb on chairs, tables, cabinets, shelves, trees, stone walls, statues, and cars, among other things. Not only can climbing be dangerous, but it can also damage property. It can bring reprimands from librarians whose bookshelves are climbed on or from Grandmother when her china cabinet is the Mount Everest of the moment!

As a parent, you realize the problems that climbing can cause, but you may have tried everything to no avail. Your child heads for anything that he thinks he can climb whenever he sees it. You may have tried scolding, threatening, and calm time, and you may even have been tempted to give him a swat to show him the pain he may suffer if he falls.

It's helpful to understand the nature of boys in this regard. As stated in Understand the Difference Between Boys and Girls (see page 21), boys are more aggressive and need to constantly test themselves. Each climb becomes a test of strength and endurance. Your job as a parent is to not only understand their need to climb but also to channel that need toward things and places that can be climbed safely.

PREVENTING THE PROBLEM

Anchor Tall Furniture to the Wall

Furniture anchors won't keep your child from climbing, but they will prevent bad accidents if he forgets the rule and climbs his bookcase or dresser.

Define What Is Climbable and What Is Not

Telling your child what can and cannot be climbed at least puts a framework around his climbing activities. Say, "No, you may not climb the cabinet, but you may climb the couch."

Make Climbing Rules

Making rules about climbing can channel a child's need to climb. Asking him "What's the rule about climbing on Grandma's furniture?" or "What's the rule about climbing at the library?" will remind him of the rule and help keep the rule in his mind during your visit to Grandma's house or the library.

Provide Places and Things to Climb

Recognizing your child's need to climb and providing climbable things and places will allow him to fulfill his needs and keep boundaries around his climbing.

SOLVING THE PROBLEM

What to Do

Remind Him of the Rules

When your child begins to climb something that's off-limits, remind him of the climbing rule. Ask him, "What's the rule about climbing here?"

Remove Him from What He Is Climbing

Simply taking him off whatever he's climbing and saying "I'm sorry, that is not for climbing," will stop the climb for the moment.

Bell the Cat

When you have a climber, tie bells to his shoes. Or if he prefers climbing in bare feet, pin bells to the back of his pants. This will let you know where he is at all times, which is crucial since you can't keep him from climbing if you aren't there to stop him.

Redirect Him Toward Permitted Climbs

When your child starts to climb something that's he's not permitted to climb, redirect him to something that he is permitted to climb. Say, "I'm sorry, you may not climb the dresser, but we can go outside and you may climb on your swing set."

What Not to Do

Don't Panic

When you see your child climbing something, rather than starting to panic and beginning yell, stay calm and quietly remove him from what he is climbing.

Don't Threaten

Telling your child that you will punish him if he climbs again will only encourage him to sneak behind your back to climb something so he can avoid getting caught. Remember, you can't see him climbing if you are not there!

Don't Guilt-Trip

Don't say, "You know that I get so worried whenever you start climbing things. You don't want to upset me, do you?" Using guilt will not motivate your child to stop climbing something, but it will lead him to do the forbidden climbing when you're not around. That way, his thinking goes, he won't feel guilty about upsetting you.

Don't Use Fear

Telling your child "If you climb up on that couch, you will fall and get hurt," won't keep him from climbing. But when he climbs and doesn't fall, it will suggest to him that what you say is not the truth.

CASE HISTORY: CLIMBING CONNOR

From the time he was able to walk, Connor tried to climb everything. Climbing up on furniture became too easy, so he began climbing onto the dining table. This frustrated Alyssa, his mother, because no matter how many times she told him to not climb or took him to calm time, Connor continued to climb up on the table. Finally, Alyssa and his father, Alan, put the dining chairs down on their backs so Connor would have to lift them upright to climb them. But the last straw came when Connor climbed his bookshelves and fell. Of course he cried, but soon he was trying to climb his shelves again. Fortunately, Alan had purchased anchors and had anchored all of Connor's furniture to the wall. Then he had to anchor all of the items in the house that were tall enough to climb because Connor was trying to climb them all.

It was when Alan lost his temper and threatened to deliver a swat to Connor's backside that Alan and Alyssa decided that they needed a new plan to teach Connor about climbing. How could they be the kind of parents they wanted to be if they were resorting to hitting their child? Both of Connor's parents told themselves that they would never threaten to hit Connor under any circumstances. Instead, because both parents realized that Connor was a climber and that there wasn't a good way to stop him, they would closely supervise his climbs. When out of the house, Connor was told the rules about what he could climb and what he could not. "What's the rule about that?" Alyssa would ask, and Connor would answer, "I can't climb that." Alyssa would then praise Connor's answer and offer to take him to the park, where he would be able to climb whatever he wanted. As a result, while Connor still loved to climb, his climbing stopped causing wars between him and his parents. They understood his need to climb, and he was willing to climb what he could and stay off those mountains that were off-limits.

Clinging to Parents

DEFINING THE PROBLEM

The image of a young child clutching her mother's legs – hanging on for dear life while she tries to shop, walk out the door, or leave daycare – is not make-believe for many parents. It's a real and emotionally draining part of everyday life. If it's part of your life, then you should resist the temptation to constantly attend to your clinging vine as you go about your day (no matter how tough that may be). If you want (or need) to leave your child with a babysitter, firmly and lovingly reassure her by telling her that you're proud of her for staying with the sitter and that you will return. Tell her that you're happy she has the chance to play with the babysitter. Even though she may cry when you close the door, your positive attitude will be contagious (as would a negative one). You'll also be a good model for her feeling okay about being separated and having a good time with other people. Provide lots of hugs and kisses during neutral times to prevent her from feeling ignored and needing to cling to you to get attention. Clinging, unlike hugging, is an urgent demand for immediate attention.

A note about the "First Grade Blues": Many children experience separation anxiety during their first-grade year. You, as well as your child, know that school is important and even mandatory, but that doesn't ease her anxiety when you drop her off at school. Read on to find ways of treating this problem. If the problem persists, seek professional help.

PREVENTING THE PROBLEM

Practice Leaving Your Child with a Sitter

To get your child used to the idea that you may not always be around, practice leaving her occasionally for short periods of time (like a few hours) early in her life. These breaks are healthy for both parents and children.

Tell Your Child What You'll Both Be Doing in Your Absence

This is good for dealing with the First Grade Blues! Telling your child what you'll be doing while you're gone gives her a good example to follow when you ask her to talk about her day's activities. Describe what she'll be doing and where you'll be while you're away so she won't worry about her fate or yours. For example, say, "Laura will fix your dinner, read you a story, and tuck you into bed. Your daddy and I are going out to dinner, and we'll be back at eleven o'clock tonight." Or say, "I need to cook dinner now. When I've done that and you've played with your lock-blocks, then we can read a story together." Or say, "While you're in school, I'll be at work. Then I will pick you up at after-school care. I know you'll have a good day."

Play Peek-a-Boo

This simple game gets your child used to the idea that things (and you) go away and, more importantly, come back. Toddlers and preschoolers play Peek-a-Boo in a variety of ways: by hiding behind their hands or some object, watching others hide behind their hands or some object, and (for older children) engaging in a more physically active game of hide-and-seek.

Reassure Your Child That You'll Be Coming Back

Don't forget to tell her that you'll be returning, and prove to her you're as good as your word by coming back when you said you would.

Create Special Sitter Activities

"Activity treats" help your child look forward to staying with a sitter instead of being upset by your absence. For example, set aside special videos, fingerpaints, games, and storybooks that only come out when a sitter comes over.

Prepare Your Child for the Separation

Tell your child that you'll be leaving and plant the suggestion that she can cope while you're gone. For example, say, "You will be having such a good time with Lisa. I know you'll be fine while I'm gone." If you surprise her by leaving without warning, she may always wonder when you're going to disappear suddenly again.

SOLVING THE PROBLEM

What to Do

Use Empathy and Understanding

Put yourself in your child's position as you try to feel the anxiety she may be showing you when she is facing the unknown. Say, "I know how you feel. But even though we can't be together for a while, you'll be okay and will have fun with the sitter (or your friends). I will see you later."

Prepare Yourself for Noise When You Separate and Your Child Doesn't Like It

Remember that the noise will eventually subside when your child learns the valuable lesson that she can survive without you for a brief time. Tell yourself "She's crying because she loves me. But she needs to learn that although I can't always play with her and I occasionally go away, I'll always come back."

Praise Your Child for Handling a Separation Well

Make your child proud of her ability to play by herself. For example, say, "I'm so proud of the way that you entertained yourself while I worked on the computer." This will further reinforce her self-confidence and independence, which will benefit both of you.

Recognize That Your Child Needs Time Away from You

Breaks from constant companionship are necessary for children and parents. So keep your daily routine, even if your child protests your doing something besides playing with her or fusses when you occasionally leave her with another member of your parenting team.

Start Separations Slowly

To teach your child independence, play Beat-the-Clock, see page 36. Give her five minutes of your time and five minutes to play by herself. Keep increasing the play-by-herself time for each five minutes of time spent with you, until she can play by herself for longer periods. Make sure that you can see her when she's separated from you. For an older child, make sure that you know where she is and that she can safely play by herself while out of your view.

Let Someone Else Take Your Child to School, to the Sitter, or to Daycare

This is another good way to deal with the First Grade Blues. Because your child has difficulty separating from you, let another caring, responsible adult regularly deliver her to school. She will discover that she can successfully separate and get along when you aren't with her.

What Not to Do

Don't Get Upset When Your Child Clings

Getting upset with your child for clinging to you won't teach her independence. Tell yourself that your child prefers your company to anything in the whole world but that it is important for her to learn how to get along with others.

Don't Punish Your Child for Clinging

Instead, follow the steps outlined above to teach her how to separate.

Don't Give Mixed Messages

Don't tell your child to go play by herself while you're holding, patting, or stroking her. This will confuse her about whether to stay or go.

Don't Make Sickness a Convenient Way to Get Special Attention

Don't make being sick more fun than being well by letting your sick child do things that are normally unacceptable. Sickness should be dealt with in a loving way with few changes in routine.

CASE HISTORY: "DON'T LEAVE ME!"

Natalie and Rick Gordon loved the party circuit so much that when their four-year-old son, Tyler, clutched both their jackets in horror when a babysitter arrived, they both discounted his feelings. They'd say, "Oh, come on, Tyler, honey – don't be a baby! We love you. It's silly for you to feel bad. We go out every Saturday night."

But Tyler wasn't comforted. He screamed at the top of his lungs, "Don't go! Don't leave! Take me!"

His clinging persisted, and the Gordons couldn't understand what they were doing wrong to make their son "punish" them whenever they wanted to leave the house. They asked themselves, "Does he really hate us so much that he wants to embarrass us in front of the babysitter??" The Gordons eventually related their frustration to their friends, the Reillys, who tried to reassure them by explaining that Tyler clung to them because he loved them, not because he hated them. The Reillys also related how they had helped their daughter adjust to their absence.

The Gordons tried the Reillys' strategy the following Saturday night. Before leaving, they prepared Tyler for their upcoming departure by saying "You'll have so much fun playing with Laura while we're at the movies. We'll be back after you're in bed, and we will come in and kiss you when we get home. We'll be here in the morning when you wake up. Laura will make you popcorn in our new popcorn maker and read you a story. Then you'll go to bed. We know you'll have a great time!" They didn't drag out their exit with tearful hugs, and they left Tyler while he was only whimpering. After this successful departure, they began to praise Tyler's being quiet during their explanations of where they were going, what they were planning to do, and how long they'd be gone. Whenever they got a good report from the babysitter, they'd let Tyler know how proud they were of his playing nicely while they were gone. "Thanks for being so calm and for helping Laura build your favorite puzzle last night," they'd say with a hug.

The Gordons were also patient. They knew they might have to wait several weeks before being able to leave to the sounds of happy feet, instead of stomping and wailing. But in the meantime, they stopped verbally attacking Tyler for any "babyish" behavior, and they reduced his crying by ignoring it.

Cursing and Swearing

DEFINING THE PROBLEM

Young children are, unfortunately, experts at repeating the choice expletives that you use to punctuate your conversations. Bad language appears to have great appeal to children because of the emotional impact that it has. Salty words also have higher reinforcement value than do many others, so when young children casually drop expletives at home, in preschool, or during a holiday meal, they create quite a stir – drawing either shock or laughter. This encourages them to use those powerful words to get attention from everyone as often as possible!

PREVENTING THE PROBLEM

Watch Your Language

The most effective way to prevent your child from hearing and repeating inappropriate language is to clean up your own language. This may be more difficult to do than it seems because linguistic habits can be very hard to change!

Substitute New Words for the Bad Ones

When you're totally frustrated, rather than yelling the word you would prefer, slip in a substitute, such as "Oh, fudge!" or "Shoes!" or "That dim thing." The new words can let you blow off steam but won't offend when your child uses them in front of others.

Monitor Places Where Bad Language May Be Heard

Make sure your parenting team watches the language that they use around your child. If Grandpa swears all the time, see if Grandpa will follow your rule about not swearing within earshot of your child.

Don't Expose Your Child to TV Produced for Adults

Adult-oriented programs continue to push the limits of language and violence.

SOLVING THE PROBLEM

What to Do

Make Rules About Language

When you hear your child swearing, tell her that using the swear word is bad manners and shows disrespect. Make it the rule that the word is not to be used.

Talk About Feelings

If your child uses swear words when she is angry, offer her the same substitute words you use. Then talk about her feelings to help her learn nonoffensive ways of expressing and reducing her anger and tolerating frustration when things don't go her way.

Refer to Empathy and Good Manners

Tell your child that the word she used is disrespectful and can hurt a person's feelings. Ask her how she would feel if she heard words that hurt her feelings, then tell her that it is best to do things that make people feel good. Using good manners accomplishes that goal!

What Not to Do

Don't Wash Out Her Mouth with Soap

Punishment of bad words simply drives the words underground. Your child will quickly learn that she can use the offending words when you aren't around to hear them.

Don't Shame Your Child

Shaming tells your child that she is a bad person when her only problem is that she has learned some bad behavior. Rather than shaming, tell her that you love her but that you don't love the word she used and that you want her not to use it any more.

Don't Give Bad Words Too Much Power

Making too big a deal of it when your child tries out an occasional bad word can give the word tremendous power. Don't get angry or upset about her use of a swear word.

CASE HISTORY: JACKSON DISCOVERS BAD WORDS

Four-year-old Jackson was bright and busy, both at home and at preschool. He could tell in detail and with much color all about the events that took place during his day. After school one day, Jackson was telling Hannah, his mother, about the game that he and his friends were playing with a ball. He then described what happened when the ball knocked over a glass of water used to clean paint brushes. "It made a really big f-~ing mess," he gleefully said, but Hannah was truly shocked by Jackson's choice of language.

"Where did you learn a word like that?" Hannah angrily asked.

"That's what Dad said when he dropped a can of paint in the garage," the frightened Jackson answered. He didn't like to see his mother upset.

"That's not a word for little boys to use," Hannah explained more calmly, "and your father shouldn't be using it, either. We don't need words like that to say what we want to say. Can you think of another word you could use?"

After thinking for a few minutes, Jackson answered, "I could say it was a big hairy mess. That's what Grandma says sometimes."

"Oh, I like that, and yes, I've heard Grandma say that, too. Jackson, I don't want you using that other word anymore. It is disrespectful and bad manners, and I know you want to show that you use respectful, good manners."

"Okay, Mom, I'm sorry," Jackson said and went off to play.

Hannah made a note to talk to her husband about his use of language!

Dawdling

DEFINING THE PROBLEM

Because time is an adult concept that has little or no meaning to young children, hurrying has no great advantages to them. Getting a child to hurry amidst all sorts of exciting distractions – such as toys, TV, or even his own shoes – seems like a lost cause. And often you are urging him to hurry to something he has little interest in, even though you do!

Because you are pressed for time and have to live by the clock, your anxiety can easily become your child's anxiety; but unlike you, he can't understand the stress he's feeling. He just knows that you are upset. Better to let him feel as if he's in control so you can avoid a power struggle. Getting angry because he's dawdling prevents you from becoming that caring adult he needs. So instead, use the following suggestions to motivate him to move to the ticking of your clock.

PREVENTING THE PROBLEM

Try to Be an On-Time Person

Tuning into an on-time person helps your child understand the importance of meeting time goals and builds his empathy for others. Saying "We must hurry to get ready so we can be at school on time and not keep your teacher waiting," motivates your child to move more quickly and helps him make the connection between being on time and preventing the impact of lateness on others.

Try to Allow Lead Time

If you're in a hurry, waiting for your young tortoise may lead you to lose your cool and be that much later. To avoid the anxiety that hurrying can create, make every effort to allow enough time to get ready for outings. Dawdling is a typical response to movement by someone who doesn't understand why hurrying is better than whatever he is currently doing.

Establish and Maintain a Schedule

Since a child needs routine and consistency in his daily life and tends to dawdle more when his routine is broken, establish time limits and a regular pattern of eating, playing, bathing, and sleeping. This will help to familiarize him with the time frame on which you want him to operate.

SOLVING THE PROBLEM

What to Do

Make It Easy for Your Child to Move at Your Pace

Ask motivating questions and play simple games to disguise hurrying. For example, encourage your child to get ready by having him guess what Grandma has waiting for him to eat for lunch at her house. Or ask your child to run to your arms when you want him to hurry along the path to your car.

Play Beat-the-Clock

Children always move more quickly while trying to beat a timer (a neutral authority) than while trying to do what you ask. Say, "Let's see if you can get dressed before the timer sounds."

Offer Incentives for Speed

For example, say, "When you beat the timer, then you may play for ten minutes before we leave for school." This lets your child see for himself that good things come to those who stay on a schedule.

Reward Movement as Well as Results

Motivate your child to complete a task by encouraging him along the way. For example, say, "I like the way you're getting dressed so quickly," rather than waiting until he's done and only saying "Thank you for getting dressed."

Use Manual Guidance

You may need to gently move your child through the task at hand (getting in the car, getting dressed, and so on) to teach him that the world goes on regardless of his agenda at the moment.

Use Grandma's Rule

If your child is dawdling because he wants to do something while you want him to do something else, use Grandma's Rule. For example, say, "When you've finished getting dressed, then you may play with your train."

Involve Him in Solving the Dawdling Problem

When children are involved in the solution, they feel they have power and control, and they can rise to the occasion. Say, "We seem to have a problem getting ready on time for school. Help me come up with a way for us to be on time." Then, praise his suggestions and tell him how helpful he has been.

What Not to Do

Don't Lose Control

If you're in a hurry and your child is not, don't slow both of yourselves down even more by giving him attention for dawdling (by nagging or yelling at him to get going, for example). Getting angry will only encourage your child to exercise power over you through his easygoing pace.

Don't Nag

Nagging your child to hurry up when he's dawdling only gives him attention for not moving. Disguise a hurry-up technique by turning it into a game, such as Beat-the-Clock.

Don't Dawdle Yourself

Getting your child ready to go somewhere only to have him wait for you tells him that you don't really mean what you say. Don't announce that you're ready to go to Grandma's house, for example, when you're not.

CASE HISTORY: DAWDLING ALLISON

Three-year-old Allison had a knack for noticing blades of grass or toying with her shoestrings instead of doing what was necessary at the moment. These behaviors were fine ways to explore her world, of course, but not when she needed to be focused on getting to school.

Grandma Harris, Allison's daily babysitter, found herself getting angry and nearly dragging her granddaughter to the preschool door. "Hurry! Stop dawdling!" she would command; but Allison was oblivious to any encouragement to do things faster than she wanted. Feeling helpless, angry, and resentful toward her favorite granddaughter, Grandma Harris finally told her daughter, Joanie, that she could no longer care for Allison. Joanie, Allison's mother, advised Grandma Harris to praise Allison's attempts at not dawdling and to ignore her when she dawdled. Joanie also encouraged her mother to offer Allison rewards for hurrying – something that came naturally to Grandma Harris, who enjoyed bringing her grandchildren presents.

Grandma Harris worked with her daughter on a plan for dawdling Allison. They decided to use Grandma Harris' smartphone timer; because Allison was only three, they planned to break down her getting ready into small segments. That way, Allison wouldn't feel overwhelmed by the goal. After Joanie left for work, Grandma Harris said, "It's time to get ready for school. Can you beat the timer getting your pajamas off? Let's see!"

"I can do that!" Allison said, and began pulling off the fuzzy flannels. Then the timer was set for tights, then skirt, then shirt, then shoes. Allison was ready in record time.

"Oh, my!" Grandma Harris exclaimed. "Look at you all dressed and ready, and we have time to play that game you wanted to play."

And so it went. Allison could soon get herself completely ready without any problem. Grandma Harris was pleased with her granddaughter's progress, lavished much praise on her little one, and began to enjoy getting her grandchild ready for preschool again. She felt more in control of the time frame in which they would both operate. And just as importantly, she learned that she and Allison could manage other problems with teaching tools, not temper tantrums!

Destroying Property

DEFINING THE PROBLEM

The line between destructive and creative play is not drawn for young children until parents etch it in stone for them. So before your child reaches her first birthday, draw the line by telling (and showing) her what she can and cannot paint, tear up, or take apart. This will prevent your budding artist from doing unintentional damage to her and others' property. However, it will be necessary for you to remind her from time to time of your rules about taking care of things. Also, boys generally engage in more rough-and-tumble play with their toys and need more supervision to protect toys from destruction, so you may need to remind them more often. But in general, you should consistently teach your child to be proud of and care for her things and let her creative juices flow in appropriate ways, such as on drawing paper (not wallpaper) or with a take-apart play phone (not your real phone).

PREVENTING THE PROBLEM

Provide Toys That Are Strong Enough to Be Investigated but Not Destroyed

It's natural for preschoolers to try to take apart and put together toys that lend themselves to this kind of activity (as well as ones that don't). To stimulate the kind of creative play you want to encourage, fill your child's play area with toys she can do something with (like stacking toys, push-button games, and so on), in addition to ones that just sit there (such as stuffed animals).

Give Her Plenty of Things to Wear and Tear

Provide lots of old clothes and materials for crafts, dress-up, painting, or other activities, so your young child won't substitute new or valuable items for her play projects.

Communicate Specific Rules about Caring for and Playing with Toys

Young children don't innately know the value of things or how to play with everything appropriately, so teach them, for example, to use crayons on coloring books, instead of on newspapers and novels. Say, "Your coloring book is the only paper you can color on with markers right now."

With regard to other potentially damaging behavior, say, "Books are not for tearing. If you want to tear paper, ask me and I'll give you some to tear," or, "This remote control car won't run anymore if we take it apart. You can take the screws out of this broken toy to see what's inside."

Supervise Your Child's Play and Be Consistent

Don't confuse your child and make her test the unacceptable waters over and over by letting her destroy something she shouldn't. Also, she won't know what to expect and won't understand if you destroy her fun by reprimanding her for a no-no that was formerly a yes-yes.

Remind Her about Caring

Increase your chances of keeping destruction to a minimum by letting your child know when she's taking wonderful care of her toys. This reminds her of the rule, helps her feel good about her behavior, and makes her proud of her possessions.

Model Caring for Things

As you take care of your own possessions, point out to your child what you are doing to make sure that your computer doesn't break, your books aren't used as a holder for a coffee cup, or your phone doesn't get damaged.

SOLVING THE PROBLEM

What to Do

Overcorrect the Mess

If your child is over two years old, teach her to take care of her things by having her help clean up the messes she makes. For example, if she writes on the wall, she must clean up not only the writing but also the walls in the room. This overcorrection of the problem gives your child a sense of ownership and caring. (It also teaches her how to clean walls!)

Use Reprimands

Give a brief reprimand to tell your child what she did wrong. Say, for example, "Stop tearing the book," and then tell her why it was wrong by saying "We want to keep our books nice so we can read them." Then tell her what she could have done instead, saying "Books are for reading. Let's read the book." These statements don't remind her of the unacceptable behavior but teach her the acceptable one.

Take Your Child to Calm Time

If you've given your child a reprimand and she destroys property again, repeat the reprimand and take her to calm time. Tell her to think about how to take care of things rather than damaging them.

Frequently Praise Your Child's Taking Care of Her Things

As you supervise your child's play, praise her following the rules and taking care of things. Say, for example, "You are coloring nicely in your coloring book," or, "You are playing so nicely with your truck. That way it won't get broken."

What Not to Do

Don't Overreact

If your child breaks something, don't throw a tantrum yourself. Your anger communicates the idea that you care more for your things than for your child. Make sure your degree of disappointment over something's being destroyed isn't out of proportion to what happened.

Don't Overly Punish

Just because your child damaged something valuable to you doesn't give you permission to damage your child. Rather than punishing her, put the valuable item away until she's old enough to understand its value.

CASE HISTORY: TIM THE TERROR

Walt and Becky Brady knew they had a destructive three-year-old long before the preschool teacher called them in for a conference. They could have bent the teacher's ear with tales of purple crayon on the yellow dining-room wallpaper, cars and trucks with wheels ripped off, and mosaics made out of pages from hardcover books. The last straw for them was when Tim used indelible markers on Becky's computer screen.

When the Bradys arrived home from their conference, the babysitter reported that Tim had drawn on the tile floor again with his crayons. "When are you going to stop all this destruction, Tim?" Walt screamed as he sent Tim to his room. A little later, the Bradys discovered that Tim had torn up three of his picture books while he was in his room.

The Bradys decided to change their approach. Instead of yelling at Tim, they required him to make amends for his destructive behavior. The next time they found Tim tearing a page from a book, they said, "Now you have to fix this book, Tim." They took him by the hand to the tape drawer and helped him tear off the appropriate amount of tape to repair the book.

Tim not only had to fix books, but he had to wash walls, scrape crayon off the tiles, and tape cards that he'd ripped. In addition, Walt began to help Tim satisfy his curiosity by having Tim help him fix things around the house. Tim was now learning about screwdrivers, wrenches, and other tools, and he was being a helper instead of a destroyer. And then an interesting thing happened: Tim seldom repeated a destructive behavior once he'd fixed the damage.

Thereafter, each time Tim damaged something, his parents explained again what he was allowed to tear and what he was not allowed to tear. The Bradys also encouraged Tim to be as responsible for his possessions as they were for theirs. Eventually, Tim began to embrace this responsibility. He beamed with pride when his parents praised his caring for his books, toys, and stuffed animals in a responsible way. And he was quick to make amends whenever he slipped back into his old destructive habits.

As Tim's behavior became less destructive, his parents still didn't expect him to care for his toys as they did for their adult toys. But they were careful to model neat behavior so Tim could see that they practiced what they preached about respecting property.

Exploring Off-Limits

DEFINING THE PROBLEM

Just getting into first gear in their first year, one-year-olds feel the joy of exploration from their toes to their teeth. They don't automatically know what's off-limits and what isn't, but by age two, they're able to make the distinction if you've set them straight. While restricting the adventures of your little explorers, keep in mind the balance you're trying to strike between letting normal, healthy curiosity be expressed and teaching what behavior is and isn't appropriate. Also See Testing Limits, page 251; and Appendix II: Childproofing Checklist, page 288.

PREVENTING THE PROBLEM

Childproof Your Home or Apartment

Keeping doors closed, stairways blocked, cabinets locked, and dangerous areas fenced off will reduce the number of times you have to say no to your child. Young children are busy establishing their independence and making their mark on the world, and they can't understand why they can't go wherever they want.

Establishing physical limitations will help you avoid unnecessary confrontations. (See Appendix I: Milestones of Healthy Childhood Development, page 280)

Decide What's Off-Limits

Decide what your child's boundaries will be and communicate this information early and often. For example, say, "You may play in the living room or in the kitchen, but not in Mommy or Daddy's office."

Put Away Valuable Items You Don't Want Broken

A toddler or preschooler will not understand the difference between an expensive vase and a plastic one. Play it safe by removing valuable items until your little one won't grab for everything despite being told not to. Even older children (and adults!) can break valuables when engaged in rambunctious play, of course.

Teach Your Child How and When She Can Go into Off-Limits Areas

Explain to your child the acceptable ways of playing in off-limits areas. Never allowing her to go into a room or across the street, for example, makes her want to do it even more. Say, "You can go into Mommy's office, but only with Mommy or another adult."

SOLVING THE PROBLEM

What to Do

Use Reprimands

Consistently reprimand your child for a repeated offense to teach her you mean what you say. Say, "Stop getting into my desk drawer! I'm sorry you're getting things out of my desk. The rule is that if you want something out of my desk drawer, you need to ask me."

Take Your Child to Calm Time

If your child gets into your makeup (and if that's a no-no), reprimand her again and put her in calm time to think about how to follow the rules and how to ask you if she wants to play with makeup.

Compliment Your Child When She Follows the Rules

Tell your child how proud you are of her for following the rules. Giving her that compliment will reward her desirable behavior with attention, which will encourage her to do the right thing again. Say, "Thank you for coming to ask me if you could get the markers out of my desk."

Teach Your Child to Touch with Her Eyes, Not Her Hands

Tell your child that she may look at the big potted plant in the living room with her eyes but not with her hands. This allows her the freedom to explore the item in a limited, controlled way.

What Not to Do

Don't Leave Guns or Knives Where Children Can Reach Them

No matter how much safety training children receive, the allure of weapons is too great to resist. Keep all guns locked up, each with its own approved trigger lock, and lock up the ammunition in a separate place that is inaccessible to children. Also, keep all knives locked away in a childproof place. Better safe than sorry.

Don't Make No-No's More Inviting by Getting Upset

If you become angry when your child breaks a rule, she'll see that she can get your attention from misbehavior and she'll be encouraged to get into trouble more often.

Don't Punish

Rather than punishing your child for being naturally curious and getting into things, teach her how to use her curiosity safely – a skill that will serve her well her entire lifetime. Instead of trying to stamp out inappropriate behavior, emphasize the positive.

CASE HISTORY: "DO NOT TOUCH!"

"Curiosity killed the cat" was the line Sophia Stein remembered her mother saying to her when she used to rummage through her mother's office desk, an off-limits place when Sophia was a youngster. Now she found her 15-month-old son, Sam, exploring off-limits lamps and plants. She knew he wasn't being intentionally naughty; he was behaving like a normal child. But Sophia didn't think her reactions to his curiosity seemed normal or showed much self-discipline. "No! Do not touch!" she would shout whenever he got into things he knew were no-no's.

Sophia eventually realized that Sam was only learning to avoid the penalty for getting caught by committing his "crimes" behind her back. So she decided to lock up things she didn't want him to touch, put breakable items out of reach, and keep an eye on him as much as possible.

"Touch with your eyes, not your hands," she said to Sam one particularly active morning when he had started taking everything out of a jewelry box she had forgotten to put on the top shelf. She removed the box and guided her son back to the kitchen, where they both had a good time taking the pots and pans out of the cabinet. They also played with the giant toy key and lockbox and several other toys that provided stimulation for his imagination and curiosity – toys that were appropriate for his age and appropriate for him to take apart and try to destroy.

Once the dangerous and expensive things were removed from Sam's reach and replaced with things he could play with safely, the Steins' household became more pleasant. Though Sophia knew she would have to continue monitoring her son's curiosity even though her house was childproofed, she let him have more freedom than before.

One day, Sam demonstrated that he was learning the rules when he pointed to her tablet computer, which he knew was off-limits, and said, "Stop! Mommy's! Do not touch!" To reward his good behavior, Sophia gave him a sealed box of rice, which he loved to shake like a rattle. Everyone's "toys" were safe!

Food Rules Conflicts

DEFINING THE PROBLEM

Many children today have special dietary needs for a variety of reasons, including health and religion. Because they don't understand why they have dietary restrictions – like no wheat, no peanuts, no pork, or no meat – children may whine, cry, get mad, and even try to sneak an "outlawed" food when it is withheld. The relationship between certain foods and stomachaches may not be as clear to your child as it is to you, and reasoning with her may not help her accept her plight.

PREVENTING THE PROBLEM

Get the Whole Family on the Same Page

When food restrictions are your child's alone, it is important for other family members to restrict their own diet in support of her to help her follow her food restrictions. Children can tolerate dietary restrictions best when they have a caring, empathetic adult in their lives.

Keep the House Free of the Restricted Food

It's better to not have peanut butter and regular bread in the house than to try to restrict their consumption. Your child can't sneak food that isn't there. Out of sight, out of mind.

Involve Friends and Your Parenting Team

It's important for others on your parenting team to know about the dietary restrictions that your child has, whether the restrictions are for health, religious, or other reasons. Before your child goes to another child's house, to school, or to her grandparents' house, the adults there must be aware of the restrictions and take care not to make the restricted foods available to your child.

SOLVING THE PROBLEM

What to Do

Use Empathy

When your child is whining and crying because she can't have a food for health reasons, tell her that you understand and are so sorry she can't have the food. Add that you are glad that she will feel good when she doesn't eat the food that makes her sick. This is best said while giving a hug; hugs are never restricted.

Similarly, when a young child is having trouble accepting religious restrictions on food, you can be empathetic while making it a teaching moment. For example, say, "I know it's hard, not being able to eat the same foods some of your friends eat. It was tough for me, too, when I was your age. But it's important that we respect our traditions and truly understand why we do this. Let's talk about that more after dinner."

Offer Substitutes

Tell your child that you're sorry she can't have peanut butter but glad she can have almond butter. And add that she can have it with her favorite jelly!

Give Praise for Acceptance

When your child accepts the restriction or accepts a substitute, praise her acceptance by saying such things as "Thank you for understanding why you can't have peanut butter," or "That was a good decision you made. Almond butter also tastes good and won't make you sick."

Give Your Child Language to Use

In helping your child accept dietary restrictions, start by saying such things as "What we can have at our house is this," when your child begs for forbidden food. Saying "What we can have..." is affirmative and feels much better than saying "We can't have that. Or help your child say, "I can have carrots," rather than, "I can't have nuts." When offered a restricted food, your child is more likely to follow her dietary rules when she can say what she can have.

Practice with Your Child

Practice is an excellent way to translate words into actions. When you give your child the words to say, it helps to practice saying them several times. For example, say, "How about some peanuts?" and coach her to answer, "I can have cashews." This can help establish a habit of thought and action that gives her language to use to remind her of what she can have.

Praise Your Child for Accepting Her Diet

Praise can help your child feel as if you are not her enemy but a caring adult. Say, "Thank you for accepting what you can and can't have. I know it's hard, but you are doing so well."

What Not to Do

Don't Give In

When your child is whining and crying because she can't have a restricted food, resist giving in by saying to yourself, "Oh, she can have the cookie just this once." When whining and crying pays off, you can expect it to be used many times in the future.

Don't Get Angry

When your child begs for a restricted food, getting angry and yelling won't teach your child how to live within her dietary restrictions. You will then become a source of stress and thus toxic to your child, instead of being a caring adult whom she can trust to keep her safe and healthy.

Don't Give Bad Substitute Foods

Because you feel sorry that your child can't have nuts, you may be tempted to give her a treat, such as candy. Substituting one unhealthy food for another is not the way to teach her to manage her diet.

CASE HISTORY: PICKY PARKER

Five-year-old Parker Ellsworth loved pasta and would have eaten spaghetti with red sauce every meal of the day if he could. He also loved bread and the dinner rolls that his grandmother made.

But then Parker became a picky eater. He would claim to be hungry, but after a few bites, he would say that he didn't want any more – even of one of his favorite foods. No matter what they did, his parents, Clair and Sam, couldn't get Parker to eat. He lost weight and became a very skinny kid. Parker also began claiming that his stomach hurt, so his parents began looking for stress in Parker's life. But his life seemed quite normal and as stress-free as any young kid's life. He loved school, had good playmates in the neighborhood, and had a good relationship with his parents and his extended family.

Clair was a nurse and began to wonder about physical causes of Parker's aching stomach. A visit to the doctor ruled out any physical problem that could be detected by gastric examination, and tests didn't reveal any celiac disease. Not satisfied with a child with chronic stomachaches and no diagnosis, Clair and the doctor agreed that removing groups of foods, one at a time, would help them discover if a particular food was creating this discomfort in her child.

Because pasta and bread made up quite a bit of Parker's diet, Clair decided to start there. When denied his beloved pasta and bread, Parker went bonkers. He begged. He whined. He bargained. He cried. And he threw the mother of all tantrums. But Clair would say, "I know you want your spaghetti, but let's try some other foods. How about some celery or an apple with peanut butter?" And if the tantrums persisted, both Clair and Sam would hold Parker and say how sorry they were that he couldn't have the food he wanted. They consistently followed their plan and discovered that Parker's stomachaches went away whenever he didn't eat any food that had gluten in it

So their house became gluten-free! Clair missed having food with gluten, but Sam also felt better. He discovered that he had a genetic predisposition to gluten sensitivity, too!

Getting Out of Bed at Night

DEFINING THE PROBLEM

Young children are famous for piping up with late-night requests for books, kisses, or milk – or for getting in bed with their parents. Remember that your child's need for sleep is very important. Although he probably asks you for those ten books and four drinks just to keep you near him, teach him that going to sleep will bring him greater rewards than will making a bedtime fuss.

If you're not sure whether your child is getting out of bed because he needs something or because he merely wants your attention (for example, if he's not talking yet or if he cries out instead of asking for something), go check on him. If he is safe and sound, give him a quick kiss and hug (30 seconds maximum) and make your exit. Tell him firmly and lovingly that it's time for sleep, not play.

PREVENTING THE PROBLEM

Discuss Bedtime Rules at a Non-Bedtime Time

Set limits for how many drinks of water or trips to the toilet your child may have at bedtime. Tell him these rules at a neutral time so he's aware of what you expect him to do when bedtime comes. Say, "You can take two books to bed and have one drink, and I'll tell you two stories before you go to sleep."

Promise Rewards for Following the Rules

Make your child aware that following the rules, not breaking them, will bring him rewards. Say, "When you've stayed in your bed all night, then you may choose your favorite story to read in the morning." Rewards could include trips to the park, playing favorite games, or other fun times together that you know your child loves.

Reinforce the Idea of Going Back to Sleep

Remind your child of bedtime rules as you put him in bed. Say, for example, "Remember, when you stay in your own bed and go to sleep, we get to go to the park in the morning. Sleep well!"

Do Bedtime Routines in Your Child's Bed

Conduct all of your pre-bedtime routines in his bed. If he decides he wants to snuggle with you for a little while, as part of his routine, do your snuggling in his bed. If his bed is still a crib, snuggle on the sofa.

SOLVING THE PROBLEM

What to Do

Stand Firm with Your Rules

Enforce the rule every time your child breaks it, to teach him that you mean what you say. For example, when you put your child back in his bed after he gets in bed with you (in violation of your rule), say, "I'm sorry that you got in bed with us. Remember the rule: Everyone sleeps in his own bed. I love you. See you in the morning."

Follow Through with Rewards

Teach your child to trust you by always making good on your promises of rewards for following the rules.

Play the "Quiet Game"

After hugs and kisses and final tuck-in, say, "Let's play the Quiet Game. See how long you can stay quiet. Shhhhhh." Then, in a whisper, say, "You are being so quiet. I'll be right outside listening." Then step outside his door and listen. Children love challenges, so he will try to stay quiet until sleep comes peacefully.

What Not to Do

Don't Neglect to Enforce the Rules

Once you've set the rules, don't change them unless you discuss this first with your child. Every time you neglect to consistently enforce the rules, your child learns to keep trying to get what he wants, even though you've said no.

Don't Give In to Noise

If your child screams because you enforced a rule about going to sleep, remind yourself that he's learning an important health lesson: nighttime is for sleeping. Time how long your child cries and chart the progress you're making in getting him not to resist sleep. If you don't respond to the noise, the crying time should gradually decrease and eventually disappear.

Don't Use Threats and Fear

Threats such as "If you get out of bed, the alligators will get you," or "If you do that one more time, I'm going to punish you," will only exacerbate the problem. Fear may keep your child in bed, but the fear may grow until your child becomes afraid of many things.

Remember, threats are never okay, and they destroy your trusting relationship with your child.

Don't Talk to Your Child from a Distance

Yelling threats and rules from another room teaches your child to yell, and it tells him you don't care enough to talk to him face-to-face.

CASE HISTORY: MAYA'S MIDNIGHT RAMBLINGS

Two-and-a-half-year-old Maya Long had been sleeping through the night since she was six months old. For the past month, however, she had been sleeping only a few hours before waking up her parents with screams of "Mommy! Daddy!" At first, Maya's parents would race to see what was wrong with their daughter, only to find her begging for drinks of water one night, an extra hug the next, and bathroom visits on other evenings.

After several weeks of these interruptions, Maya's weary parents decided to put a stop to these requests. "If you don't stay in bed, you're going to be punished, young lady," they threatened. Then they returned to their bed, only to hear their daughter padding down the stairs toward their room. Their heavy hand seemed to carry little weight.

The Longs kept telling themselves that Maya's waking up in the middle of the night was natural – everyone went through periods of shallow and deep sleep. But they also knew that their daughter could choose to go back to sleep instead of calling out to them. They also felt confident in their ability to distinguish between a genuine distress call (an intense and uninterrupted cry) and one that merely sought their attention (short bursts of crying punctuated with listening pauses).

To solve the problem, they offered Maya more attention for staying in bed. "Here's the rule: when you stay in bed without calling out to us," they explained as they tucked her into bed the next night, "then you'll have your favorite surprise at breakfast in the morning." They made sure they stated the new rule in plain terms that their daughter could understand.

That night, Maya called out for her mother, "I want a drink!" But her mother followed through with her promise of no surprise at breakfast the next morning. After three nights of this pattern for the Longs, Maya learned that calling out did not bring her parents to her bedside and that staying quiet and in bed all night made the promised surprises materialize in the morning. The Longs were finally able to get some uninterrupted sleep, and Maya found that their praise for sleeping through the night made her feel grown-up and important – an extra reward.

Gun Pretend-Play

DEFINING THE PROBLEM

Many moms and dads lament the fact that little boys, in particular, love to turn every object they touch into a weapon. From baseball bats to carrots, they pick up found objects and use them to simulate weapons, often using them to imitate what they see on TV (with boys being more affected by violent TV than are girls). Young children do not process information in the same way as adults do, nor do they have the tools to evaluate what they see. (See Understand the Difference Between Boys and Girls, page 21)

It has been reported that young children who were given guns and other violent toys to play with acted more aggressively than did those who only watched a television program with violent content. But studies have also shown that by the age of three, children will imitate someone on TV as readily as they will a real person. The results of the studies on the effects of viewing television violence are consistent: children learn how to be aggressive in new ways and draw conclusions about whether being aggressive will bring them rewards.

Those children who see television characters getting what they want by using weapons are more likely to imitate those acts themselves. If parents approve of their children's use of weapons or exhibit violent behavior themselves, they serve as negative role models of violence for their children. (See Section Three, page 25) On the other hand, parents who show their children how to solve problems nonviolently and who consistently praise their children for finding peaceful solutions to conflicts are positive role models of how to be less aggressive.

So when your young child makes pretend guns out of french fries, don't panic but don't ignore his imaginative play, either. Instead, teach the important lesson that even pretending to physically hurt people can upset people. Keep in mind that the behavior of the adults closest to a child encourages him to be kind or cruel. Watch what you do and say – and how explosively you act – in order to help curb your child's appetite for violent play.

PREVENTING THE PROBLEM

Make Caring a Household Rule

When your child behaves aggressively, make a rule that tells him what is or isn't allowed regarding his pretending to use toys in violent ways. For example, say, "The rule is, 'We treat people nicely to show them that we care.' Pointing guns, even pretend ones, is against our family's rules because it upsets people and makes them afraid."

Think Before Speaking

Use words and a tone of voice that you wouldn't mind your child repeating. For example, when he breaks a rule, instead of threatening (even in jest) to "knock his head off if he doesn't stop," calmly say, "I'm sorry you decided not to follow the rule about pretending to use a gun. The rule is, 'We treat each other nicely and don't ever hurt or pretend to hurt anyone.'"

Model Kindness

You are your child's first and most important role model. When you listen to, hug, apologize to, and respect your child, he will learn to behave the same way with others.

Learn to Control Your Anger

What causes children to "go off" is the same thing that causes adults to explode: anger over something beyond their control. Tell yourself you hope that you get a raise, the traffic is light, your favorite dress still fits, and so on. But if none of these wishes comes true, don't have a meltdown. By keeping your cool, you set a powerful example for your child of regulating your emotions when things don't go your way.

SOLVING THE PROBLEM

What to Do

Teach Empathy

When your child pretends to attack another person with a toy gun or other object, consider this a teachable moment. Ask him to think about how it would feel to be shot by a pretend gun. Say, "Guns can hurt people. How would you feel if someone acted as if he were going to shoot you? I wouldn't want to scare or hurt anyone. I hope you wouldn't want to, either."

Encourage Cooperative Play

Children who learn to enjoy building things, sharing with others, and engaging in supervised social activities will have less opportunity to resort to violent games for entertainment. Praise your young child when he's getting along with others while playing so he knows you approve of his playing nicely. Say, "I like the way you're getting along and being kind to each other by sharing toys."

Restrict Violent TV and Video/Computer Games

It is well documented that young children like to imitate what they see. Many children have been victimized by playmates who use in "real life" the kicks and punches that they see their favorite characters use in fictionalized television programs or video games. Strong identification with a violent television character and believing that the television situation is realistic are both associated with greater aggressiveness. You need to know what your child is watching and what games he's playing. Reduce the amount of violent content your child is exposed to by making a rule about what he can watch or what games he can play, as well as about how long he can watch or play. Put yourself in charge of access to screens to keep violence out of your home and out of your child's imagination. (See Too Much Screen Time, page 262)

When Your Child Uses Screens, Watch with Him

To help a child become an educated viewer, it's important for you to be there to discuss what he sees on any screen. For example, if a character is being bullied, it allows you to point out what bullying behavior is, its effect on the victim, and the lesson that bullying someone in real life hurts and is harmful (even though it might not seem so in the program on electronic media).

Teach Your Child to Make Amends

When an overly exuberant tot tries to "shoot" a sibling or playmate with a ruler, take away the "weapon" and reprimand your child by saying "Guns hurt people. The rule is, 'We treat each other kindly and never even pretend to hurt another person.' We don't hurt people; we love people. Please tell Sam you're sorry for pointing a gun at him." When your child follows your directions, say, "Thank you for being Sam's friend. I like the way you're showing him that you care about him."

Reduce Aggression by Teaching Your Child to Compromise

Help your child learn to resolve disputes peacefully. When you see him threatening to hit his friend for taking his toy, say, "Let's think about what else you could do when your friend takes your toy and you want it back. You could get the smart-phone timer and set it like I do so your friend can play with the toy for a while and then you can play with it. That way, both of you get to play with it and have fun."

What Not to Do

Don't Hit!

No matter how tempting it is to spank a child to "smack some sense into him" or "teach him a lesson," resist the urge. Although you may be angry and scared when your child crosses the street without your permission, spanking him for doing so sends him a mixed message: It's okay for me to hit you but not for you to hit me or anyone else.

Practice what you preach. Spanking teaches him it's okay to hurt people to get them to do what you want, as well as many other lessons that you don't want your child to learn. (See Section Three, page 25) Even the occasional swat on the behind sends the hurtful message that if you're bigger and stronger, it's okay to hit to make a point. Studies have also shown that three-year-olds who are spanked twice a month will be almost 50% more aggressive than non-spanked children by age five.

Avoid Overreacting

When your child pretends to shoot his little brother with his pencil, remain calm. Instead of simply forbidding the behavior, take advantage of a teachable moment by saying "I'm sorry you broke the rule about treating people kindly. Pretending to shoot your brother is mean and disrespectful. Tell me the rule about how to treat people and show me how you can treat your brother with respect."

Don't Threaten

Threatening to hit your child with a wooden spoon when he's pretending to hit his sister with his stuffed animal only teaches him to fear your presence. To your child, a threat is an empty promise and an example of how adults don't keep their word. So instead of threatening a violent consequence such as "I'll give you a spanking if I see you pretending to shoot your brother with that empty paper towel roll again," simply say, "I'm sorry you chose to break our rule about pretending to hurt someone. Now I want you to think about how scared you'd feel if somebody pointed a gun at you."

CASE HISTORY: "SCARY" KYLE

No matter what he got his hands on, three-year-old Kyle Liggett made it into a gun, knife, or sword. Then he shot, stabbed, or slashed away at any "bad guys" who were around. Kyle's mother, Diane, was beside herself. She was convinced that if she didn't bring play weapons into the house, her son wouldn't play so violently. Miles, Kyle's dad, only laughed about her fears. "Oh, Diane, boys will be boys. Why, I had toy guns when I was a kid, and you don't see me going around acting like I'm going to shoot people."

"But he makes a weapon out of everything," Diane lamented. "Today at lunch, he bit his peanut butter and jelly sandwich into a gun and pretended he was shooting it at me. It was scary to see the mean look on his face as he was pointing the 'gun' at me."

"You should spank him when he does that," Gary responded. "That'd teach him not to point even a pretend gun at anybody."

"I'm not going to spank him," said Diane indignantly. "It doesn't make any sense to hurt him to try to teach him not to hurt people. I was talking to Amy, Josh's mom, and she said that they got Josh to think about how others feel when a gun's pointed at them. She also made a rule that all violent media were not welcome in their home. The screens went off whenever Josh chose that kind of garbage. She told me that he got the message."

"Well, let's try the same thing," Miles suggested. "By the way, I just thought about something else I should stop doing. You know how I'm always saying stuff like 'If you do that once more, I'll rip your arm off!' I guess that sends Kyle the message that if a person is mad at someone, it's okay to hurt him."

Over the next few weeks, Kyle's parents squelched their violent messages. Instead of threatening him when he played pretend shoot-'em-up, they said things like "I'm sorry you're choosing to point guns at people. Guns can kill, and pointing guns at people scares them. Let's play school with that ruler, instead of pretending to hurt somebody with it. Put the ruler on this paper and see what a straight line you can draw with your markers."

"It's amazing," Diane told Miles. "I've been catching Kyle every time he uses a pretend gun and showing him something else to do with it. Now he's saying 'Mommy doesn't like watching that,' whenever he sees somebody hurting someone on TV."

Miles laughed and said, "I overheard Kyle playing with Josh, and when they started to pretend they were shooting each other, Kyle said, 'It's not nice to point guns at people. It hurts their feelings. Let's play with my trucks and stuff.'"

Kyle wasn't allowed to pretend to shoot someone at home, nor was he allowed to do so at preschool, church, or anywhere else. Although the Liggetts didn't believe that Kyle truly wanted to hurt someone, they knew that others might not be so sure of his motives. They wanted Kyle to understand that life is precious and it's wrong to hurt people, messages that they hoped every child would be fortunate enough to hear from a loving parent.

“Hyper” Activity

DEFINING THE PROBLEM

“Jackie’s so hyper!” her grandmother exclaimed after two hours of grueling babysitting with her young granddaughter. “She wouldn’t sit down once – not even to eat!” Jackie’s mother had heard the term *hyper* used before to describe her daughter, but when Jackie’s grandmother started complaining about Jackie’s behavior, Jackie’s mother asked herself, “Is Jackie a normal, busy two-year-old, or is she hyperactive?”

Clinical tests must be done to obtain a proper diagnosis of hyperactivity, but even this may not be definitive for young children. If you see four of the symptoms below in your child on a daily basis for at least six months, consult a professional trained in diagnosing hyperactivity:

1. Fidgeting frequently
2. Leaving her seat
3. Running or climbing excessively
4. Having problems playing quietly
5. Being constantly on the go
6. Being overly talkative

7. Blurting out answers before the question is completed
8. Having trouble waiting in lines or taking turns
9. Interrupting or intruding on others

A professional can help you understand the difference between a "hyper" active child and a hyperactive child – and she can help you manage the behavior of both. Because these behaviors often describe the average young child, it's very difficult to attach the label "hyperactive" to a little whirling dervish.

Hyperactivity is considered part of a larger disorder commonly referred to as Attention Deficit Hyperactivity Disorder (ADHD), which comes in three forms: 1) ADHD, Predominantly Inattentive Type; 2) ADHD, Predominantly Hyperactive/Impulsive Type; and 3) ADHD, Predominantly Combined Type. All forms of ADHD are difficult to diagnose before children enter formal schooling at about age five – when they're first required to sit and pay attention for longer periods of time, work while remaining seated, and memorize material that they'll be tested on later. Boys tend to be more active than girls, so avoid comparing males to females. (See Appendix III: Is My Child Hyperactive?, page 291)

PREVENTING THE PROBLEM

Suggest Quiet Activities

If your child regularly runs instead of walking and screams instead of talking, introduce calm activities to slow her breakneck speed. For example, play the QuietcGame, read to her, or have a tiptoe-and-whisper time to teach her that "slow and calm" is a refreshing change of pace.

Watch Your Own Activity Level

Does hyperactivity run in families? Research has shown that when a parent is diagnosed with hyperactivity, it's highly likely that his or her child will be, too. But look at your own life: Do you ever sit down? Do you talk fast? Is your pace always rushed? If you're a high-energy, always-on-the-go person whose "hyper" activity doesn't get in the way of your success and happiness, then your child may simply have your inborn temperament. Since young children are such great imitators, slowing down your activity level will show your young child how to savor the moment.

Provide Plenty of Activity Options

Young children have short attention spans and seem to flit from one activity to another, always demanding something new to do. "Hyper" active children need even more play choices because they are always on the hunt for something to stimulate their ever-hungry brains. Being able to guide your child to a new exciting activity before she has an energy explosion will eventually help her learn to guide herself.

Avoid "Hyper" Active Screen Time

When your child is in constant motion, her entertainment shouldn't be. Frenetic television programs and video games model behavior you don't want her to emulate. Depending on your child's age, limit her exposure to TV and video games. (See Section Two, page 9) Instead, play quiet, restful music and encourage more restful activities, such as reading.

SOLVING THE PROBLEM

What to Do

Practice Slowing Down

Give your child opportunities to practice walking – not running – from Point A to Point B. Say, "Show me how to walk from the kitchen to the family room. I know you can do it. When you walk instead of run, you keep yourself safe." Gradually increase the number of practice walks to a maximum of ten each practice session.

Provide a Variety of Activities

Born-to-be-busy children flit like summer houseflies from one activity to another and have trouble staying in one place. Give your "hyper" active child a cafeteria of choices by saying "You can color on your drawing table, play with clay in the kitchen, or play with your building blocks. I'll set the timer on the phone, and you can do one activity until the timer rings. Then you can choose something else if you want." Providing many options lets your child fulfill her need to be busy without driving you to distraction.

Exercise

Your high-energy child needs constructive outlets for her need to be on the go. Let her run in the park or in your yard whenever you can, or make sure her school or daycare provider gives her some running time.

Although it may be tempting to sign her up for the neighborhood sports team that all her buddies are on, beware of starting your young child too early in sports that can injure her growing body or cause her to burn out. Young children need the freedom to rev up their newly charged engines without being corralled in an organized, competitive setting.

Teach Relaxation

When your child learns to relax her body, her motor slows down and she feels less frantic. Help her avoid constantly pushing to do more, go faster, or get there sooner by keeping your voice soft and soothing, by rubbing her back, and by talking to her about how calm and relaxed her body feels.

Seek Help

If your child's "hyper" activity endangers her health, alienates others, and jeopardizes her learning, consult a trained professional to determine the cause of her above-average activity level. (See Appendix III: Is My Child Hyperactive?, page 291)

What Not to Do

Don't Punish

When your "hyper" active child accidentally collides with your most precious vase, take a deep breath and say, "I'm sorry you chose to run instead of walk. Now you have to practice walking in the house so I'll know you can do it. Then we'll clean up the mess." In this way, you'll reach your ultimate goals of teaching your child to walk instead of run, respect property, and be responsible for her own actions.

Don't Ground

Your busy child needs daily opportunities to play in the great outdoors, so grounding her to the house or her room can cause two problems: (1) her "hyper" activity will swell to explosive levels, and (2) she will only learn to be hyper in the house instead of outside.

Don't Rely on Medication Alone

Relying on medication alone won't teach your child self-control. Get a thorough evaluation from a professional experienced in assessing "hyper" active children before you decide what behavioral tools and/or medications are necessary for your child's well-being.

CASE HISTORY: WILD ABOUT ETHAN

When Jane and Russell Anderson attended Ethan's teacher conference at school, they weren't at all surprised at Ms. Sharon's comment that their five-year-old son was very active.

"He even kept me awake at night when I was pregnant with him, he was so restless and busy," Jane told her. "When Russell is out of town, I let Ethan sleep with me, and it's the same thing. I don't get much sleep because he's so restless. He never walks; he runs. He's just like his dad." Jane put her hand on Russell's knee, which had been in constant motion since he first sat down for the conference.

"Yeah, I was a hyper kid," Russell grinned. "Mom had to go to school lots to bail me out because I was always in trouble for being out of my seat, talking, or doing something stupid. I had to take medication to calm down. Do you think Ethan needs medication?"

"Well, it's not such a big problem in school now, so I don't think medication is called for. But it would be good to keep an eye on him," Ms. Sharon told them. "When he's in first grade next year, you should work closely with his teacher to see if something more needs to be done. In the meantime, here's a list of things you can do to try to slow him down a bit, as well as the best places you can go for a full evaluation. We believe that children should have a thorough evaluation before starting any kind of medication or treatment program."

Jane and Russell took the list home and began working with Ethan. Several times a day, they had quiet time during which they read stories to him or relaxed with him. At first, Ethan couldn't sit still for more than 50 or 60 seconds, but gradually, he began to sit for ten minutes at a time. They also cut out most of the TV Ethan liked to watch and imitate – from wrestling mayhem to martial arts – after his teacher suggested limiting his exposure to such frantic fare.

His mom and dad also made a new household rule: "When you're in the house, you must walk. Running is for outside." To teach him the rule, they had Ethan practice navigating the house by walking. This was new to Ethan.

"But what if I'm in a hurry? Why can't I run if I want to?" Ethan whined.

Jane smiled inside at Ethan's question. She remembered having to help Russell learn how to slow down after he knocked over a lamp one night trying to get to the kitchen and back before a TV commercial was over. "Because it's against the rule to run in the house," she answered. "Running is for outside, where you have lots of room to run and won't bang into the furniture."

Jane also started doing simple relaxation exercises with Ethan at bedtime. She rubbed his back while softly saying "You're feeling quiet and relaxed. Your feet feel heavy and relaxed. Your legs, your tummy, your back, your arms, and your hands all feel relaxed and comfortable. Your whole body is relaxed and warm. Your mind is quiet, and you're comfortable and still. Now – Ethan, my love – think of being in your bed all quiet and snuggly while you're feeling so calm and quiet."

Ethan gradually became calmer and quieter and somewhat less active. It wasn't always easy for him to keep his body quiet, but he worked at it with his parents and his teacher, which helped prepare him for making a smooth transition to the less active world of the first grade.

Ignoring Requests

DEFINING THE PROBLEM

Sometimes it seems as if your young child might have lost his ability to hear – because when you tell him to do something, there is no response! Then you ask again, this time louder. Again, no response. And the next thing you know, you are so frustrated that you begin to yell your request. But your child still ignores you.

If the scene above sounds familiar to you – and if you have a child who cannot hear your voice but can hear the rustle of a candy wrapper in a distant part of the house – take heart, you are not alone! Young children can become absorbed in an activity to the extent that everything else around them disappears, which isn't a bad thing. This "selective hearing" is a skill that will stand them in good stead when they enter school and have to concentrate while the teacher conducts a reading group nearby, for example.

However, your young child may simply be ignoring you because he doesn't *want* to do what you asked him to do. He may also not want to shift from what he's doing to what you've asked him to do. Young children don't like to shift activities because they want to take what they are doing to completion. On the other hand, if you suspect that your child is ignoring your requests because he may have a hearing problem, check with his healthcare provider.

PREVENTING THE PROBLEM

Make Eye Contact with Your Child Before Making Requests

Ensure that your child hears you when you speak by getting down on his level, lifting his face so you can see his eyes, and then speaking.

Make Requests Simple and Short

Your young child can only absorb a limited number of words at a time. He may not actually be ignoring you but may simply be unable to process all of the information you are giving him in your request. So just tell him one thing to do and wait for him to do the task before giving him another instruction.

Keep Your Voice Calm and Quiet

If you are always yelling, your child will shut out your voice because it is annoying and meaningless to him. The softer the voice you use, the closer the attention that your child has to pay to hear your instructions.

Prepare Your Child for the Request

Your child may be reluctant to shift to a new activity, so warn him a few minutes before you make your request. This will allow him to prepare. Say, "I will set my phone timer to ring in a minute. That will tell you that you need to get dressed for school."

SOLVING THE PROBLEM

What to Do

Have Your Child Repeat the Request Back to You

Once you've made eye contact and have made a short request in a quiet voice, ask your child to repeat the request back to you. Say, "Now, what did I ask you to do?" If he can't repeat the request, tell him again.

Use Grandma's Rule

Remember, Grandma's Rule states that your child may do what he wants to do when he has done what you want him to do. Say, "When you have your school clothes on, then you may finish the puzzle."

Play Beat-the-Clock

Set a phone timer for a reasonable time and say, "Let's see if you can beat the clock as you get your pajamas off." When that task is complete, say, "Let's see if you can beat the clock getting your pants on." Then go for the sweater and then the socks and shoes. Remember, small and short requests work best.

Praise, Praise, Praise

You can praise your child's behavior frequently during the task by saying "Thank you for looking at me while I talk," or "Thanks for listening," or "Look how quickly you are getting your pajamas off," or "You are getting dressed so fast. You're going to beat the clock." This kind of encouragement will keep your child interested and moving to complete your requests.

What Not to Do

Don't Get Angry

Getting angry when your child doesn't listen doesn't teach him how to listen to you. It just creates stress in your relationship and inside you and your child.

Don't Threaten

When your child repeatedly ignores your requests, don't say, "If you don't pay attention to me right now, I'm going to take all of your toys and throw them in the trash!" This threat may frighten him enough to get his attention, but it doesn't teach him to listen and do what you ask. In addition, it provides a model of bullying someone to get what you want – the model that you don't want him to follow to get his needs and wants met.

CASE HISTORY: EMMA LEARNS TO LISTEN

Sarah was tired of four-year-old Emma's totally ignoring her when she asked her to do something. Sarah had tried to be nice about being ignored, but then she lapsed into what her mother had always done when she was little: yelling, threatening, and then snatching her daughter up and stomping with her to whatever task she had asked her to do. She had even asked Emma's pediatrician whether she should have Emma's ears checked to see if she had hearing loss. The doctor assured her that Emma's hearing was fine.

Sarah then took some time out to think the problem through. She decided that Emma was ignoring her because she wasn't able to shift easily to a new activity. Having her Mom demand that she stop and move on didn't give her the sense of completion that she needed. Wow! What a concept, and one she had arrived at herself as a young child! Sarah remembered that her mother and she had clashed because Sarah had hated having to stop immediately and do what her mother wanted. Sarah had always felt good inside when she finished a project that she had started.

So now that she understood the reason for Emma's listening problems, she had to develop a strategy. Sarah decided to give Emma a warning before she asked her to do something. She would give her this warning while she was right next to Emma and touching her gently. So she tried it, saying "Emma, in a minute, you're going to have to put this book away and brush your teeth. I'll set the cell phone timer to remind us when a minute is up." When the phone chirped, Sarah went back to Emma, saying "Emma, it's time now to put the book away. Let's see if you can do it before I count to five. One, two, three..."

Emma quickly closed the book and put it with the others. "See, I did it before you finished counting!" Emma squealed. "I knew that I could!"

"Emma, you are so fast. I am excited about how quickly you did what I asked you to do. Now let's get your teeth brushed so we can read stories before bed. How many stories tonight?"

"Five stories." Emma said as they headed for the bathroom.

Sarah and Emma went through the same kind of routine, getting teeth brushed and into bed for stories. Sarah decided that Emma needed a little time to shift into a new activity rather than being forced to jump into it immediately.

Impatience

DEFINING THE PROBLEM

Because patience is not an innate virtue for everyone, young children must be taught the art of waiting for what they want. They also must learn to accept that they may not always get their own way. Your young child is just discovering that the world will not always revolve around his desires, so it's not too soon for him to start learning how to cope with this often frustrating fact of life.

PREVENTING THE PROBLEM

Explain How Being Patient Can Be Rewarding

Because you have your child's best interests at heart, you can help him learn the payoff of patience. Explain the conditions clearly. For example, say, "I know you want to eat the cake batter, but it's not good for you. When you wait until the batter is baked, it will turn into delicious cake for you to eat."

Provide a Menu of Activities from Which Your Child May Choose

Set up conditions that must be satisfied before your child gets his own way, and provide him with suggestions for activities he can do while he's waiting for what he wants. For example, say, "Let's think about what you can do while you wait. You may read a book, play with your trucks, build with the interlocking blocks, go outside to the swing, or help me put the clean clothes away."

Set Firm Boundaries

If your young child knows that you have set boundaries on his behavior and you will stick to those rules, he will be more likely to follow your rules. For example, if he asks to skateboard in the street, say, "I know skateboarding in the street looks like fun, but that's against the rules. You may skateboard on the sidewalk, but you must stay out of the street."

SOLVING THE PROBLEM

What to Do

Encourage Patience

Reward even the slightest sign of patience by telling your child how glad you are that he waited. Define *patience* if you think he might not be familiar with the word. For example, say, "You're being so patient by waiting calmly for your drink until I clean the sink. That shows me how grown-up you are." This teaches your child that he does have the ability to put off his wants, even though he doesn't know it yet. It also helps him feel good about himself because you feel good about his behavior.

Remain as Calm as You Can

If your child protests waiting or not having things his own way, calmly remind yourself that he's learning a valuable lesson for living: the art of patience. By seeing you be patient, he'll soon learn that being demanding doesn't get his wants satisfied.

Use Grandma's Rule

If your child is screaming, "Go! Go! Go to the park!" simply state the conditions he must meet to satisfy his wants. Be positive. Say, "When you've put the books back on the bookshelf, we'll go to the park."

Avoid Always Giving a Flat "No" to Things Your Child May Not Have or Do

Whenever it's possible and safe, use Grandma's Rule to tell your child how he can have his own way. For example, say, "When you've washed your hands, then you may have an apple." Sometimes, of course, you need to say no to your child – when he wants to play with your carving knife, for instance. At those times, try to offer alternative playthings to satisfy his wishes and to foster a sense of compromise and flexibility.

Share Your Personal Experience

Show your child how having patience pays off in your life, too. Say, for instance, "I know it's unpleasant for me to wait to buy the new dining-room furniture I want, but I know that if I work hard at saving money, I'll be able to buy it soon."

WHAT NOT TO DO

Don't Demand That Your Child Do Something "Now"

Demanding that your child immediately do what you want contradicts the lesson you're trying to teach. If you don't want him to demand instant results, don't do it yourself.

Don't Reward Impatience

Don't give in to your child's desires every time he wants his own way. Although it may be tempting to do so in order to avoid a battle or a tantrum, constantly giving in only reinforces his impatient behavior and fails to teach him patience.

Make Sure Your Child Knows It's Not His Demanding Behavior That Got His Wants Fulfilled

Though your child may moan and groan throughout the waiting time, make sure he knows that you are getting in the car because you're ready and your jobs are done, not because he wailed his way out the door. Say, "I've finished washing the dishes. Now we can go."

CASE HISTORY: "I WANT IT NOW!"

"Drink now!" two-year-old Emily Randolph wailed every time she was thirsty. When she saw her mother giving a bottle to her new baby brother, Justin, she wanted one, too – immediately.

"No, I'm busy. You'll just have to wait!" her mother, Aria, responded, growing impatient with her daughter for not understanding that babies don't know how to wait for what they want. But Emily made so many demands to be held or given toys or drinks that Aria Randolph began to dread the moment when Emily would enter the room, especially while Aria was taking care of Justin. When Emily began taking food, drinks, toys, and blankets away from Justin – saying that they were "mine" – Aria realized that she needed to fix the problem.

Aria declared a new rule, called Grandma's Rule, and explained it to Emily: "When you do what I ask you to do, then you may do what you want to do. This is the new rule." That afternoon, Emily insisted on having a drink only ten minutes after the last one. Aria stated firmly, "When you put your shoes on, then you may have some apple juice." Emily was used to hearing "No," and then throwing a tantrum until her mother gave in, so she ignored the new rule and continued to cry and scream as always. But not only did her tantrum not bring a drink, it caused Aria to ignore Emily completely. The frustrated girl finally put on her shoes to see if that would bring her the attention (and drink) she wanted, since screaming had not. She was surprised and delighted when it did.

Emily quickly learned that her mother meant what she said, because she never strayed from enforcing Grandma's Rule. When Emily fulfilled her part of the bargain, Aria praised her accomplishments with comments like, "I'm so glad you cleared the dishes from the table. You may go outside now." Aria's admiration was sincere, and Emily appreciated it and became more responsive to her mother's rules, which Aria tried to limit whenever possible. As the family learned to work together to satisfy everyone's needs, they grew to enjoy living with – not in spite of – each other.

Interrupting

DEFINING THE PROBLEM

Because a young child's most priceless possession is his parents' attention, he'll try anything to get it back when they are on the phone, computer, or tablet, or if another person takes his parents' attention away. Limit the tricks your child tries to play to get your undivided attention by providing him with special playthings, activities, and other alternatives to your attention that are reserved for those times when you're chatting with "the competition." This will keep your child busy without you, while you're busy without him.

PREVENTING THE PROBLEM

Limit Your Distractions When You Are with Your Child

Your child has a limited ability to delay gratification, so when you are with your child, keep the distractions at a minimum (see Section Two, page 9) to prevent interruptions that are frustrating to you both.

Actually Be There!

It's frustrating when you are with someone but he is not "with" you because he is texting, tweeting, checking email, or engaged with his friends online. And your child is no exception. When he wants your attention, he will get it by interrupting your texting, tweeting, and not paying attention to him. This is the time to teach a child that it is not polite to interrupt but that it is also disrespectful to ignore someone who is standing right in front of you.

SOLVING THE PROBLEM

What to Do

Praise Playing Nicely and Not Interrupting

If your child is getting attention (smiles, praise, and so on) for playing and not interrupting, he'll be less inclined to barge in on your conversation. Excuse yourself momentarily from your conversation and say to your child, "Thanks for playing so nicely with your toys. I'm so glad that you are having fun on your own."

Whenever Possible, Involve Your Child in Your Conversation

When a friend visits, try to include your child in your conversation. This will reduce the possibility of his interrupting you to get attention.

Thank Your Child for Not Interrupting

After you and your child have your separate "playtimes," praise his respectful behavior and reward him by playing with him. Say, "Thank you so much for playing with your toys while I worked on the computer. That was so helpful to me to get some of my work done. Now we can play your favorite board game."

Use Grandma's Rule

Use the timer on your phone to let your child know that you'll soon be all his again. He can earn your attention and have fun at the same time. Tell him, "When you've played with your toys for two minutes and the timer sounds, I'll be through talking to my friend and I'll play with you."

Reprimand and Use Calm Time

Use a reprimand such as "Please stop interrupting. I cannot talk to my friend while I'm being interrupted. Instead of interrupting, please play with your cars." If your child continues to interrupt, use calm time to remove him from the possibility of getting attention for interrupting. Say, "I'm sorry that you're continuing to interrupt. Time for calm time."

What Not to Do

Don't Get Angry and Yell at Your Child for Interrupting

Yelling at your child about any behavior only encourages him to yell and doesn't teach him how to give you interruption-free time.

Don't Interrupt People, Especially Your Child

Even if your child is a constant chatterbox, show him that you will not interrupt him while he's talking. Be a role model of the behavior you want him to learn.

CASE HISTORY: "NOT NOW, RILEY!"

Whenever Amelia Wilkens talked on the phone, was on social media, was texting, or was trying to do work online, her three-year-old daughter, Riley, interrupted with requests for drinks of apple juice or toys from the "high place." She also asked questions like "Where are we going today?"

Although Amelia wanted to answer, she tried to explain calmly at each interruption, saying "Sweetheart, Mommy is busy. Please don't interrupt." But Riley continued to interrupt, so one day Amelia started screaming in frustration and anger "Don't interrupt me! You're a bad girl!" Not only did the yelling not shut Riley up, it angered her into crying and screaming so loudly that her mother couldn't continue her own activity. The more her mother yelled, the more Riley interrupted – a cause-and-effect situation that Amelia finally understood and decided to reverse.

She realized that she needed to give her daughter attention for *not* interrupting instead of for interrupting. The new plan started when Amelia's friend Maria texted her the next morning, as she did every Monday morning. Amelia was busy exchanging texts with Maria, but she took a moment to notice how Riley had begun playing with the toys that Amelia had gathered around the sofa where Amelia was sitting. "Thanks for not interrupting!" she said to Riley, giving her a big hug. When she finished texting with her friend, Amelia again praised Riley's behavior, saying "Thanks for not interrupting me while I told Maria about our dinner tonight. These markers are here for you to play with, if you want." The toys were especially fascinating to Riley because they were called special-time toys – ones she was allowed to play with only when her mother was busy at home.

The next time they heard the ringtone, both Riley and her mother smiled with anticipation. Amelia said, "Riley, that's my phone. Let's play with the special-time toys." Riley ran to get the markers. While talking on the phone, Amelia watched Riley carefully and encouraged her noninterruptive behavior with an occasional, "Nice playing." As they put the markers away later, Amelia praised Riley for showing respect during the phone conversation.

Jealousy

DEFINING THE PROBLEM

Young children live at the center of their own universe, so they believe they should get undivided attention whenever they demand it. This self-centered view of life is the source of sibling rivalry and jealousy. When the attention they demand isn't there because it's being given to a new baby, another sibling, or even a parent, young children often morph into green-eyed monsters. Smitten with jealousy, they sulk, sabotage, scream, or solicit more attention by hitting their siblings, breaking toys, throwing tantrums, and so on. Justified or not, your child's jealousy can tear your heart out. Interpret her jealous behavior as a teachable moment by giving her both the attention she needs and the opportunity to be helpful. (Also see Sibling Rivalry, page 226)

PREVENTING THE PROBLEM

Keep Your Child Involved

While you're changing your baby's diaper, for example, enlist your other child's help by asking her to get a new diaper, hold the lotion, or entertain the baby. If your young child becomes jealous while you're hugging your hubby, a bigger hug to include her can put the wind back into her sails.

Praise Sharing

When your child accepts that your attention's being directed elsewhere, point out her willingness to share by saying "That was so nice of you to share me with the baby. Thanks for being so generous."

Help Your Child Feel Special

To keep the green-eyed monster at bay, allow your older child to help open the baby's gifts and show them to the baby. Encouraging friends and relatives to bring gifts for both children helps keep the older child feeling special.

Try to Give Even Amounts of Attention to Siblings

Although you may not be keeping a tally of the minutes of attention you give to one child or the other, your jealous one certainly is. Be aware of your little accountant and refocus on her – after you've been talking to her brother, for example – to keep her attention-getting misbehavior at a minimum.

SOLVING THE PROBLEM

What to Do

Show Empathy

When jealousy flares, tell your child you understand how she feels by saying "I know you don't like it when I have to take care of the baby, but I think you can handle it. After you play with your building blocks until I'm through, I'll play with you."

Provide Alternative Activities

Understand that your child gets jealous because she feels left out when you and your partner want some time together. Give your child something constructive to do until you're ready to give her your undivided attention. Say, "Daddy and I want to talk for a while. You can play with your toys until the timer rings. Then you can talk to me if you want."

Monitor Your Time

To a child, love is spelled T-I-M-E. Consider how much time you spend with your child reading stories, answering questions, sharing meals, playing games, and so on. When your child feels secure in your love, her jealousy meter stays low because she knows she's your number one priority. Tell her "I love you" many times each day. Strengthen your bond with each of your children by making special play dates for just you and her so each child feels valued and important.

Turn Jealousy into Helpfulness

A young child wants her world to exist for her alone, but she also wants to be independent. By teaching young children to be helpful toward siblings and others when they are feeling left out and jealous, you're helping them turn negative behavior into something positive and praiseworthy. Say, "I know you want me to play with you now, but first I have to take your brother to soccer practice. Come help me put the oranges in the sack so the boys will have a treat. You can have one, too."

What Not to Do

Don't Compare Your Child to Siblings or Others

Saying "I wish you could be as helpful as your little brother," or "Why can't you be as sweet as your big sister?" only tells your child that she's not living up to who you want her to be. To children, that translates into not being as lovable as other family members, which is a sure-fire way to stir up the green-eyed monster.

Don't Punish

When your child gets out of sorts because she wants your undivided attention, punishing her for being upset will only increase her sense of alienation. Instead, show her how she can better cope with not getting the attention she wants when she wants it. Say, "I'm sorry you're so upset because I can't play right now. Let's make a deal. I'll play with your baby sister for a while, and when the phone timer rings, I'll read your book to you. Next time, we'll switch and you can go first."

CASE HISTORY: GREEN-EYED GRACE

Grace Goodman was really excited when she learned that she was going to have a baby brother or sister. She loved the idea of having a new playmate, which seemed to her like a new toy. Her parents, Sam and Christine Goodman, were convinced that Grace wouldn't have any problems accepting the new baby. But were they in for a surprise!

Everything went well the first few days after Baby Jayden was brought home, because Grammy was there and Grace got lots of attention. Grace told her mom and dad that she thought Baby Jayden looked funny, didn't smell very good sometimes, and wasn't able to play with her like she wanted. But she reassured her mom by saying "I guess it's okay if he stays. Let's keep him for a while."

However, when Grammy left to go back home – a 1,000 miles away – Grace realized that her mom had to spend way too much time taking care of Baby Jayden. Grace decided she needed to reassert herself as the number one kid in her house. She tried whining for a while, but that didn't make her mom leave Baby Jayden and come play with her. Then she tried sulking, but nobody seemed to pay any attention to that, either. So she started refusing to do what her mom and dad asked, like putting away her toys or brushing her teeth. Her mom was exasperated by this change of attitude and said, "Grace, what's gotten into you?"

When Sam came home that evening and heard what Grace had done, his first response was, "Oh yes, the green-eyed monster has come to visit. Your mother warned us this might happen."

So the Goodmans developed a plan to involve Grace in caring for Baby Jayden. Grace became Mommy's Little Helper and was eager to assist when Baby Jayden was being changed or fed. She even held the storybook so Christine could read to her while feeding Baby Jay.

When Grammy came to visit, she brought Grace a little gift as well as one for Baby Jayden. Grace got to open Baby Jayden's gift so she could show him what Grammy brought. Grammy also spent plenty of time with Grace so she didn't feel so left out when Grammy was holding Baby Jayden.

Like a miracle, green-eyed Grace became a much more pleasant child to have around. The Goodmans knew that their empathy for Grace helped her accept the new family member and the important responsibility of being a big sister.

Lying

DEFINING THE PROBLEM

Young children live in an interesting world where fantasy and reality mix. They enjoy cartoons, pretend play, Santa Claus, wicked witches, flying capes, make-believe on demand, and so on. Their storytelling often reveals hidden fears. For example, shouting "Mommy, there's a monster in my room! Come save me!" may be your child's way of telling you she's afraid of the dark. Also, young children can be convinced of almost anything. If they want to believe something badly enough, they can convince themselves of the truth in even the biggest lie.

Lying signals another step toward independence, as fledglings stretch their wings and push away from parental control. So what's a parent to do? Your job is to understand the flavor of the lie and sell your child on the benefits of telling the truth. Knowing that the truth is important to you will make being honest more important to your child. It is easier for your child to tell the truth when you are a caring adult she knows she can trust.

PREVENTING THE PROBLEM

Reinforce Telling the Truth

Offer praise when you know you're hearing the truth, whether it's about something bad that happened or something good. This helps your young child begin to understand the difference between what's true and what's not.

Model Telling the Truth

When your young child asks for a cookie right before dinner, you might be tempted to say, "We don't have any more cookies," instead of telling her the truth, which is "I don't want you to eat a cookie before dinner." By lying to her, you're telling her that it's okay to lie when she wants to get out of doing something unpleasant. She knows where the cookies are, so don't pretend that she doesn't! Say, "I know you want a cookie now, but when you've eaten your dinner, you can pick one out yourself."

Learn the Flavors of Lying

Lying comes in a variety of flavors. Plain old vanilla is the one we all know so well: lying to stay out of trouble. "I didn't take the last cookie" is a good example. A more pungent flavor is lying to get out of doing something you don't want to do. For example, your child might say, "Sure, Mommy, I brushed my teeth," when she hasn't. And then there's the ever-popular, extra-smooth lying that gets whipped up when children try to impress others with comments such as "I have three horses that I get to ride every day. So there!"

Be Empathetic

Understand the flavor of lying that your child is using and respond accordingly. For example, when your child tells you that she didn't mark her bedroom wall with crayons even though you know she did, tell her "I understand that you don't want to be punished, but I'm more disappointed that you chose to lie rather than tell the truth. You can always tell me the truth so we can fix the problem together." Your child will feel more comfortable facing the music and telling the truth when she knows you'll be sensitive to her feelings.

Look for Honesty

Look for people and events that demonstrate honesty and truth. Point these out to your child to reinforce your message that being honest is important. And don't forget to praise your child's honesty.

SOLVING THE PROBLEM

WHAT TO DO

Show How Lying Hurts

When your child is caught in a lie, explain to her how it hurts her as well as you. Say, "I'm sorry you chose not to tell the truth. It makes me feel sad that I can't trust what you say. Let's work on telling the truth so I can believe that what you tell me is true. Telling the truth helps me trust what you say."

Explain the Difference Between Lying and Telling the Truth

Young children don't always know that what they're saying is a lie because it might seem like the truth to them. Help your child understand the difference between reality and fantasy by saying "I know you want your friend to like you, but telling him that you have 101 Dalmatians living at your house isn't truthful. The truth is that you'd like to have all those dogs, but you only have one dog named Molly. She's a really nice dog, and you love her a lot."

Help Your Child Accept Responsibility

When you ask your daughter to do a chore such as putting the toys away in her room, she might lie to get out of doing the job by telling you that she already did it. Say, "I'm so glad you did what I asked. I'll go see what a great job you did."

If she says, "Oh no, Mommy, not yet," you can be reasonably sure she's avoided her responsibility. Check it out! If you discover that she lied, say, "I'm sorry you chose not to tell me the truth about doing what I asked. I know you didn't want to put all those toys away and didn't want me to be disappointed, but doing what I ask and telling the truth are important. Now let's go get the job done. I'll watch while you pick up."

Practice Telling the Truth

When your child lies to you, she's letting you know she needs practice telling the truth. Say, "I'm sorry you didn't tell me the truth when I asked you if you had turned off the TV. Let's practice telling the truth. I want you to say, 'Yes, Mommy, I'll turn off the TV when this show is over.' Now let's try it."

Play Make-Believe with Your Child

To help your child understand the difference between truth and fiction, set aside time for her to make up stories. Then contrast this *story time* with *truth time* in which she's asked to tell the truth about what happened. When your child tells you something that you know isn't true, say, "That's an interesting make-believe story you just told me. Now tell me a true story about what really happened."

What Not to Do

Don't Test Your Child's Honesty

If you know your child has done something wrong, asking her a question to which you already know the answer forces her into a dilemma: tell the truth and get punished or lie and maybe get away with it. Don't make her choose.

Don't Punish

When you catch your child lying – for example, by saying that she didn't use a pencil to draw on the walls when she actually did – don't punish her for lying. Instead, teach her how to accept responsibility for making a mistake and to fix the problem it caused. For example, say, "I'm sorry the wall has marks on it. Now we're going to have to learn about taking care of walls. Let's get the cleaning stuff and start cleaning. I'll get the cleaner while you get the paper towels. Telling me the truth about marking on the walls lets us fix the problem."

Don't Model Lying

Avoid exaggerating or making up stories to impress people, to avoid consequences, or to get out of doing what you don't want to do.

Don't Overreact

Even if you've said to your child a 100 times that you can't stand a liar, going ballistic when your child lies only forces her to avoid telling the truth to keep you from getting mad.

Don't Label Your Child a Liar

Don't make lying a self-fulfilling prophecy. A child who's called a liar will believe that what she does is who she is. Your child isn't what she does. You might not love her behavior, but you'll always love her unconditionally.

Don't Take Lying Personally

Little Dana isn't telling you an exaggerated version of her morning at daycare just to make you crazy. She may actually believe that the classroom's pet snake got out of its cage because she was so scared that it would. Listen to her story and tell her, "That's an interesting story, sweetheart. I'm sure having the snake loose in the room would be really scary. Do you want me to talk to Ms. Laura about keeping the snake safely locked up in its cage?"

Don't Talk a Lot about Lying

Talking about lying just keeps what you don't want in front of your child instead of what you do want. Talk about telling the truth, which is the behavior that you are trying to teach your child.

CASE HISTORY: "DON'T YOU LIE TO ME!"

Although Ryan Kirk had just turned four years old, his parents had already tagged him as a liar. He'd come home from preschool and tell Julie, his mother, the most fantastic stories about how somebody broke into his school and held everyone hostage; how his teacher had been told she couldn't work there anymore; or how his friend Adam had brought his pony to school. Every day, it was something new, and Julie was becoming afraid that Ryan's fantasies were getting out of hand.

Lawrence, Ryan's dad, had also heard Ryan's tall tales. He had recently confronted his son about some juice that had been spilled in the kitchen, and the answer he got astonished him. Ryan tried to convince his dad that someone broke into the house to steal stuff and must have spilled the juice on the floor. "But son, it's the same grape juice that you have in your cup right now. How do you explain that? Now don't you lie to me!" When Ryan didn't have an answer, he was sent to calm time so Dad could calm down and Ryan could have some time to think about telling the truth.

Julie and Lawrence soon realized that this consequence would not teach their son to tell the truth, because the more they took him to calm time, the more he lied. He even tried to lie his way out of calm time. Ryan's parents loved him and needed to help him understand that they would love him no matter what happened. They also knew that their son didn't have to lie to impress them or to stay out of trouble, but they weren't sure if he knew that. When they thought about how the world seems to little children – a confusing blend of fantasy and reality – the Kirks understood that they could help their son by teaching him the difference between truth and fiction. They decided to change their problem-solving strategy.

"Tell me about school today," Julie said when Ryan got into the car after preschool the next day.

"Well," Ryan began, "today was real neat because the football team that plays in the stadium came and showed us how to play football; but Josh got hurt and they had to take him to the hospital in an ambulance..."

Then Julie stopped him. "Wow!" she exclaimed. "That must have been exciting. Is this what you wanted to happen today at school, or did this really happen?"

"Well..." Ryan answered, "I wished it had happened. Then school would have been more exciting."

"Ryan, your story was very interesting, but I really want to know the truth. You don't have to make up things about school so I'll think your day was exciting. You can tell me about the games you played, who sat next to you at snack time, what Ms. Sharon talked about, and all sorts of things that I'd like to hear about. I have an idea. You like to make up stories, so let's have story time when you can make up stories, and then let's have truth time when you can report what actually happened during your day."

So Ryan got into the habit of saying "Story time, Mom." Then he'd launch into a fantastic tale about his day at school, and they'd both laugh. Julie would rave about how much she enjoyed story time.

"Now it's truth time, Ryan," his mom would then say, and he'd report on the more mundane events of the day. Julie would tell Ryan how much she loved his truth time tales, too. This allowed Lawrence and Julie to accomplish three goals: they taught their son lessons in honesty, taught him how important telling the truth was to them, and supported his budding storytelling creativity.

Mealtime Meltdowns

DEFINING THE PROBLEM

You may often find yourself pushing your on-the-go young child to eat. But your child may be too busy investigating her world to take much time out for food. The bottom line is this: don't make a fuss about food! Also, young children are notorious for their occasional bouts of not wanting to eat, so don't mistake these for illness. However, get professional help if you think that your child may be physically ill and unable to eat.

PREVENTING THE PROBLEM

Don't Skip Meals Yourself

Skipping meals gives your child the idea that not eating is okay for her since it's okay for you.

Don't Emphasize a Big Tummy or Idolize a Bone-Thin Physique

Even a three-year-old can become irrationally weight conscious if you show her how to be obsessed with her body.

Learn the Appropriate Amount of Food for Your Child's Age and Weight

Consult your child's healthcare provider for answers to specific nutrition questions about your child. For more information about recommended guidelines for young children, consult the website Choosemyplate.gov.

SOLVING THE PROBLEM

What to Do

Encourage Less Food, More Often

Although you may want to provide only three meals at particular times of day, your child's stomach can't hold enough food to last four or more hours between meals. Let your child eat as often as she likes, within limits. Be mindful of when a main meal is coming when you provide snacks, and only offer the best foods for good nutrition. Say, "Whenever you're hungry, let me know and you can have celery with peanut butter or an apple with cheese." Make sure you can follow through with your suggestions, based on what foods are available and what time a main meal is coming.

Let Your Child Choose Foods

Let your child choose her between-meal snack or lunch food (with your supervision). If she feels she has some control over what she's eating, she may be more excited about food. Offer her only two choices at a time so she doesn't become overwhelmed with the decision-making process, and praise her choices with comments like "I'm glad you chose that orange. It's really a delicious snack."

Provide Variety and Balance

Children need to learn about proper diet, which involves a wide range of foods. Expose your child to the various tastes, textures, colors, and aromas of nutritious foods. Remember that children's tastes often change overnight, so don't be surprised if your child turns down a food today that was a favorite last week.

Grow Your Own Veggies

If you have space for a small garden or can use large pots for planting, try growing a few vegetables. Children who have a hand in growing food are often more willing to try foods they ordinarily turn down.

Let Nature Take Its Course

A normal, healthy child will naturally select a balanced diet over a week's time, and pediatricians say this will keep her adequately nourished. But she will do this only if a wide variety of healthy foods is available. Make a note of what your child has eaten from Monday through Sunday before becoming alarmed that she's undernourished.

Establish Regular Mealtimes

Because your child is not on the same eating schedule as you are, she may often want to play outside or finish an art project when your mealtime arrives. Identify the times when your child seems to get hungry to learn what kind of hunger clock she's on (which you could switch to, if possible). She may need to be trained to switch to your schedule for sitting together, or you may choose to switch to hers. The bottom line is this: meals are healthiest, emotionally and physically, when they are fun times for family interaction.

Table Time Rules

Encourage your child to interact with you at the table for a reasonable amount of time for the child's age. Say, "The smartphone timer will tell us when dinner is over. The rule is that we want all of us to stay at the table until the phone timer rings. Tell me when you're finished eating and I'll remove your plate."

This is an important distinction: Your child doesn't have to keep eating to stay at the table with you – just as with adults! The point is that you want your child to be at the table to get her accustomed to this healthy habit that she will follow for the rest of her life: mealtime is a time to satisfy "social hunger" as well as physical hunger.

What Not to Do

Don't Bribe or Beg

When your child is not eating, don't bribe or beg her to clean her plate. This makes not eating a game to get your attention, which gives your child a feeling of power over you.

Don't Get Upset When Your Child Won't Eat

Giving your child attention for not eating makes not eating much more interesting to her than eating.

Don't Overreact

Downplay the attention you give to your child's not wanting to eat. This will keep eating time from becoming a battleground on which you wage power struggles.

CASE HISTORY: "I WON'T EAT!"

When Owen Rowland turned seven years old, his appetite dropped to zero. His parents, Leo and Lillian, didn't know why – and neither did his pediatrician, who checked him over physically at the insistence of Owen's fretful mother. One night, after Lillian had begged him to eat just one pea, Owen threw a vehement tantrum, pushed his plate off the table, and shouted, "No, I won't eat!"

Leo decided to take over this mealtime battle. "Now, Owen, listen to me. If you don't take a bite of macaroni, you'll have to leave the table," he threatened, firmly letting his son know the rule of the moment. But he never guessed that Owen would take him up on the offer and get down from his chair. "Owen Rowland, you will not get down from this table!" Leo yelled. "You will stay and eat your dinner if you have to sit here all night," he said, changing the rules and thoroughly confusing his son.

Later that night, after they had kissed and hugged their son and put him to bed, the Rowlands decided that something different had to be done. They did not want to yell at their little boy for not eating. They wanted to turn mealtime back into what it used to be – a time for food and fun exchanges of stories, songs, and the events of the day – because they understood how important family dinnertime is. So the next night at dinner, they shifted their attention away from food and pretended to ignore Owen's lack of appetite.

"Tell me about how you were the helper at school today, Owen," his mother began (with all the sincerity and calmness she could muster) as she passed the broccoli to her husband. Owen perked up as he told the story of how he was chosen to hold the flag. In between his excited explanations, he just happened to swallow a forkful of mashed potatoes. "That was so nice of you to be such a good helper today," Lillian complimented her son. "I'm glad you like the mashed potatoes, too," she added. The Rowlands continued their meal but refrained from pushing their son to try a few more potatoes.

The next morning, Owen's parents discussed the evening's success and decided to continue what they were doing. They also remembered what Owen's doctor had said: "Owen may eat only small amounts, judging from his normal but slight body size, and he may eat those more than three times a day, as many people do."

Dinnertime became less of a daytime preoccupation for Lillian. She began creating fun carrot-stick boats and cheese-and-raisin faces for Owen to eat throughout the day. Owen developed a whole new interest in eating more during the day, though he still only took a few mouthfuls at dinner. But the Rowlands appreciated those minutes Owen did spend eating, and they let their son dictate when he was and wasn't hungry.

Mealtime Messiness

DEFINING THE PROBLEM

Take a one-, two- or three-year-old, mix her with food she doesn't want to eat, and presto! You have an instant mess on your hands, her hands, and probably the floor and table, too. Children are little researchers who sometimes like to experiment with food to see what happens. It is fun to watch peas roll across the kitchen floor, and the mashed potatoes make such nice snowflake designs when dropped on the floor. And oh, the milk! Such a glorious mess!

When your child starts playing with her food instead of putting it in her mouth, it usually means she's finished eating, whether she can say the words or not. Consistently take her food away as soon as it becomes a weapon or a toy, even if she's still hungry. This will teach her that food is meant to be eaten, not played with.

PREVENTING THE PROBLEM

Don't Play with Food Yourself

If you play with the food on your plate while talking or after you're finished eating what you want, your child will assume that she can do it, too.

Serve Food in a Form She Can Handle

To reduce the likelihood of a mess, cut her food into bite-size pieces that are easily handled and chewed.

Keep Bowls of Food out of Reach

To avoid messes, steer playful young children away from the temptation to serve themselves from a larger serving dish or pitcher.

Teach Your Child Table Manners at a Non-Eating, Neutral Time

Your child needs to know what you expect of her in restaurants and at home. It's best to teach her these expectations when you're not actually sitting down to dinner. For example, have frequent "tea parties" where you show her how to use her spoon, keep food on her tray, keep her hands out of her food, tell you when she's finished eating, and so on. Say, "When the smartphone timer rings, you may leave the table. Please tell me when you're finished and I'll take your plate."

Talk to Your Child at the Table

If you make conversation with her, she won't find other ways to get your attention, such as playing with her food.

SOLVING THE PROBLEM

What to Do

Teach Your Child Your Rules about Playing with Food

Tell your child that her plate will be removed when she plays with her food. And calmly explain that she will be required to clean up any mess she makes in playing with her food at the table before it's taken away. For example, when she playfully pours her milk on the table, say, "I'm sorry that you made a mess with the milk. Remember the rule. Now you need to clean up the mess. Here's a towel to use. I will show you how to use it."

Compliment Proper Eating Habits

Anytime your child is not playing with her food at the table, tell her you like how well she's using her manners. Say, "I like the way that you're twisting that spaghetti around your fork as I showed you to do."

Ask Whether Your Child Is Finished When She Starts Playing with Her Food

Don't immediately assume that your child is being playful with her food. Ask her if she is finished eating when she is dissecting her meat loaf, for example.

What Not to Do

Don't Lose Your Cool

Though you may be disgusted and angry at your child for playing with her food, your anger may be the spice she wants with her meal. Your little one thrives on having the power to affect the world (for better and worse).

Don't Let Playing with Food Become a Way of Getting Attention

Ignore any food play that is not harming anyone else and that you feel comfortable accepting at the table. So for example, ignore arranging peas into a smiley face, but don't ignore throwing food at others.

Don't Give In

If you remove the food because your child is playing with it, don't put it back just because she has a tantrum and screams that she wants it. Teach your child that you will follow through with your rule that if she plays with her food, you will remove her plate.

CASE HISTORY: DINNERTIME DISASTERS

Dinnertime at the Langners' was looking more like art class than mealtime since five-year-old Nick had begun smearing food around his plate and spitting out what didn't tickle his taste buds. His parents, who were disgusted with their son's wasteful games, tried to stop him by screaming "Don't play with your food!" But even after his mother threatened, "If you do that with your peas one more time, I'll take you down from the table," Nick tried to roll one more pea down the slope of his fork. Clearly, threatening to take him from the table didn't stop him from playing with food.

So the Langners decided that Nick must not need to eat all of the food that they put on his plate. When he was full, he simply used his leftover food for entertainment! Nick's parents began to anticipate when he was full. They trained themselves to notice when his playful eyes and hands started to find new things to do with his french fries and green beans, and they quickly removed his plate. Nick's mother also spent a few minutes during the day teaching her son to say, "I'm through now," which he could do to signal when he was finished eating.

Both of Nick's parents were relieved after experiencing three straight weeks without any food "art" at the table. But then Nick chose to try his hand at smearing creamed corn on the table. Fortunately, they had decided what the rule would be for slip-ups, and they calmly explained it to Nick: "Whenever you make a mess, you must clean it up." Instead of yelling at Nick, they calmly demonstrated the process.

Nick didn't get any attention for having to clean up his mess by himself, and it took only three wipe-up nights for him to start saying "I'm through now." Those words worked like magic, he discovered, and he appreciated the hugs and kisses from his parents, who would say, "Thanks for saying 'I'm through now,' Nick. I know you're finished with your dinner, and now you may go play with your trucks."

The whole family seemed relieved that more time was spent talking about how nicely Nick was showing good manners at the table, instead of about how destructive he was with his food. Dinners with their son were shorter and sweeter than ever before.

Messiness (General)

DEFINING THE PROBLEM

Little people make big messes! Unfortunately for orderly parents, young children are almost always oblivious to their self-made clutter. Know that your child isn't deliberately being messy but is simply unaware of the need to clean up after himself. Teach him (the younger the better) that, as much as we wish it were true, messes don't disappear magically – the mess maker (with helpers) cleans them up! Share this fact of life with your child, but don't expect perfection in his following the rule. Encourage, rather than demand, neatness by praising the slightest attempt your child makes at playing the cleanup game.

PREVENTING THE PROBLEM

Model Neatness

If you don't clean up the kitchen after you cook, hang up your towel after a shower, or put away clothes after they're washed, you are providing a model of messiness – which is not exactly the goal you have for your child's behavior. Even if it's a lesson you don't take seriously yourself, try to change your priorities to help your child make cleanliness a priority.

Clean as You Go

Show your child how to put away his toys immediately after he's finished playing, to limit clutter as he bounces from plaything to plaything. Help him pick up the picking-up habit early in life, to encourage him to be a neater child and, later, a more organized adult.

Show Him How to Clean Up His Mess

Provide appropriately sized bins and containers in which your child can store his toys and other playthings. Show him how to fit her things inside the containers and where they go when they're filled. This way, he'll know exactly what you mean when you ask him to put something away or clean something up.

Be as Specific as You Can

Instead of just asking your child to clean up his room, tell him exactly what you'd like him to do. For example, say, "Let's put the pegs in the bucket and the blocks in the box." Make it as simple as possible for your child to follow your instructions.

Provide Adequate Cleanup Supplies

Don't expect your child to know what to use to clean up his mess by himself. For example, give him the right cloth to wash off the table. Make sure to praise all his cleanup efforts after you've given him the tools of the trade.

Confine Messy Activities to a Safe Place

Avoid potential catastrophes by letting your child play with messy materials (finger-paints, clay, markers, crayons, and so on) in appropriate places. Don't expect him to know not to destroy the living-room carpet when you've let him fingerpaint in there.

SOLVING THE PROBLEM

What to Do

Use Grandma's Rule

If your child refuses to clean up a mess he's made, make his fun dependent on doing the job you've requested. For example, say, "Yes, I know you don't want to pick up your blocks. But when you've picked them up, then you may go outside to play" Remember that even a child who is just becoming mobile can help clean up in small ways. He needs to try his best at whatever level he can, slowly building up to more difficult tasks.

Work Together

Sometimes the cleanup job is too big for a young child's muscles or hands. With a positive attitude, join in the work to encourage building a supportive relationship through sharing and cooperation – two lessons you want your child to learn as a young child. Seeing Mom or Dad clean up makes the activity that much more inviting.

Play Beat-the-Clock

When your child is trying to beat the smartphone timer, picking up toys is a fun game instead of an arduous task. Join in the fun by saying "When you've picked up the toys before the timer sounds, you can take out another toy." When your child is successful at beating the clock, praise his accomplishment and follow through on your promise.

Praise Your Child's Cleanup Effort

Encourage your child to clean up after himself by using a powerful motivator – praise! Comment on the great job he's doing putting away his crayons, for example. Say, "I'm really glad you put that red crayon in the basket. Thanks for helping clean up your room."

WHAT NOT TO DO

Don't Expect Perfection

Your child hasn't had much time to practice cleaning up after himself, so don't expect his job to be perfect. The fact that he's trying means he's learning how to do it. He'll improve over time.

Don't Punish Messiness

Punishing him for being messy will not teach him the cleanup skills he needs to learn.

Don't Expect Young Children to Dress Themselves for a Mess

Your child doesn't understand the value of nice clothing, so provide him with old clothes (and put them on inside out, if you want) before allowing him to play with messy materials.

CASE HISTORY: MULTIPLE MESSES

As parents, John and Mandy Wareman were getting used to everything but the messes their five-year-old twins, Harper and Hannah, made almost daily. "Good children always put away their toys," Mandy told them, trying to convince the girls not to leave their toys in the living room when they were done playing. When that didn't work, she began yelling at her daughters and putting them in their rooms when they didn't clean up their mess. But that punishment seemed to punish only Mandy herself, because the girls created additional messes while in their rooms.

Mandy finally saw a way to solve the problem by using Grandma's Rule when she realized how much her children liked to play outside on their new swing set. She decided to turn that activity into a privilege that had to be earned. One day, the girls wanted to go outside instead of cleaning up after playing with the pegs and the kitchen set. Using Grandma's Rule, Mandy said, "Here's the new rule, girls: I know you want to go outside. When you've picked up your kitchen set, Harper, and your pegs, Hannah, then you can play on the swing set. I will help."

The two girls looked at each other. They didn't want to pick up their toys, but they really wanted to play on the swing set. Mandy began helping put the pegs in the jar to make sure that Hannah knew what cleaning up the pegs meant. Mandy also opened up the bag so Harper could deposit the kitchen utensils in their proper place, leaving no doubt about what "picking up the kitchen set" meant.

As the girls began cleaning up, Mandy let them know how happy she was with their efforts. "Thanks for cleaning up," she said." You're doing a great job filling that jar with pegs. I sure like the way that kitchen set fits into that tiny bag." She hugged each girl with genuine pride. Soon, both children spilled out the door, leaving their mother to fix lunch instead of clean up after them.

For many weeks, the girls needed to be motivated by Grandma's Rule to clean up. But they finally learned that putting away one toy before taking out another made the cleanup process quicker and also brought great compliments from Mom.

Noise Problems

DEFINING THE PROBLEM

Young children are naturally noisy creatures who generally lack awareness of how quiet they need to be in different places. They may talk loudly during religious services, shout excitedly when they find a familiar book at the library, and dance and sing to the annoyance of neighbors directly below their apartment. You may have lectured and threatened, but your child's short attention span and natural exuberance keep the noise around. It is important for you to teach your child that some places are quiet zones, but don't expect her to always remember, without your prompting, all the places that are quiet zones.

PREVENTING THE PROBLEM

Pick Your Setting

Understand that young children are natural noise machines, so avoid putting them in situations in which they need to be quiet until you know that they can follow your quiet rule. If, for example, you've been invited to a solemn ceremony, understand that your child may not remember to use her "indoor voice" and will make noise. Make other arrangements for her if you want to avoid the inevitable.

Keep Visits to Quiet Places Short

You know how tedious it is to have to spend a long time in a quiet place, and you are an adult! From a two-year-old's perspective, five minutes of behaving quietly may be intolerable. Plan being in quiet zones for as brief a time as possible.

Shoes Off

If you are an apartment dweller and have downstairs neighbors, make it a rule that all shoes are left at the door. Stocking feet make a little less noise than shoes, and that can help soften the sounds that your neighbors hear coming from your apartment.

SOLVING THE PROBLEM

What to Do

Establish Rules

When going to a quiet zone, tell your child that the rules are to stay quiet, stay close, listen, and whisper.

Practice

Before going to the library, remind your child of the rules by saying things like "Remember that the library is a quiet zone. We need to use our quiet voices while there. So now let's practice. Pretend that we are in the library. Put your finger on your lips so you'll remember to be quiet."

Leave the Quiet Zone

When the quiet rule is consistently violated, even after your reminders to use the quiet voice, realize that it is important for you to respect others and practice the quiet-zone behavior at home before bringing your child to the quiet-zone spot. Say, "I'm sorry you won't stay quiet. We have to leave now." This may cause a momentary outburst, but it's important to follow through and leave as promised.

Play the Quiet Game at Home

Set your cell phone timer for three minutes and say, "Let's stay as quiet as we can until we hear the ring sound." Whisper praise to your child during the time period by saying such things as "You are behaving so quietly." Gradually increase the quiet time until you are comfortable with your child's understanding that she can behave quietly.

Model Quiet

Your child needs frequent examples of the behavior you expect of her, so be sure to show her how you want her to behave. When at home in your apartment, for example, try to use your quiet voice all the time. In addition, your child will listen more attentively when you use a quiet voice.

Plan Quiet Activities

When you want your child to be quiet for a limited amount of time, you should have quiet activities available, such as picture books, markers and paper, or an electronic tablet upon which your child can read/draw or play an educational game to keep her interest focused. Save the loud activities for the playground.

What Not to Do

Don't Yell

No matter how frustrated you feel, avoid yelling. Not only is it an ineffective way to help your child learn appropriate behavior, but it models the exact opposite behavior from the quiet you want her to exhibit.

Don't Go Places You Know Your Child Can't Handle

Because you understand that your child has difficulty staying quiet in quiet zones, don't set her up to fail. Try not to go to quiet zones until you know that she has learned to follow the quiet rules when needed.

CASE HISTORY: LOUD LUCAS

Five-year-old Lucas was loud. He loved to run, jump, and yell as he let his exuberance run wild. But Lucas lived with his mother in an apartment, and the noise he made often brought complaints from the people who lived in the apartment under them.

Try as she might, Lucas's mother, Laura, could not keep him contained. She found that she was constantly reprimanding him for being too loud, and her anxiety level was soaring as she thought about her neighbors. Laura threatened Lucas with a spanking if he made noise, but she knew how wrong it was to hit her young son. So calm time became her only tool, and Lucas seemed to be spending more and more of his time at home sitting in a little chair waiting for the timer to ring. Laura was pleased that she could keep Lucas quiet for most of their time together at home, but she knew that having him sit in calm time all the time wasn't good for him or for their relationship.

Laura decided to try a new strategy that she thought might teach Lucas how to keep himself quiet for longer periods of time while at home. She decided that outside activities would be Lucas's reward for being quiet, as well as a safety valve for the steam Lucas built up while being quiet. So on a Saturday, when Lucas was jumping up and down while begging to go to the playground, it was time to implement Laura's plan. She told Lucas that they could go to the playground when he could stay quiet for half an hour so she could get the breakfast mess cleaned up. Laura set her phone timer and gave Lucas some choices of quiet activities that he could do while waiting. Lucas chose playing with his interlocking blocks.

During the kitchen cleanup, Laura frequently complimented Lucas on how quietly he was playing, and she reminded him of the playground trip that he was earning. However, after 15 minutes, Lucas began jumping off the couch to topple the building he had made.

"Lucas, I'm so sorry you weren't able to stay quiet until the timer rang," she said. "Now we have to start all over, and your blocks are too noisy now. Please choose another activity."

Laura reset the timer for 30 minutes and Lucas chose the block catalog to look at while he waited. He would frequently come to the kitchen to ask about different sets he was seeing in the catalog, but he walked quietly and was complimented for being quiet.

This time, Lucas won the Quiet Game and earned a trip to the playground. Laura decided to use the timer more when they were home, and she made a list of quiet activities they could do together. She decided that evenings would be mostly spent playing together with Lucas until his bedtime, after which she could get her work done. As a five-year-old, he needed her to help him structure his time and learn to use self-control when he needed to become a more quiet version of himself!

Not Doing What They Are Told

DEFINING THE PROBLEM

Young children love testing limits, which tests the patience of every adult they encounter during their early years. They are curious to see whether their parents will follow through on their warnings, how far rules can be stretched, and how closely directions *really* need to be followed.

To answer all of these questions, give your child consistent results from her research on the adult world. Prove to your child that you mean what you say so she will feel more confident about what she can expect from adults in her world. Your making and enforcing rules may seem dictatorial to your child, but despite her protests, she will feel more secure growing up knowing the boundaries on her behavior that your rules and limits establish.

PREVENTING THE PROBLEM

Learn How Many Directions Your Child Can Follow at Once

Your young child will only be able to remember and follow a certain number of directions at a time, depending on her developmental stage. To find out your child's limit, give one simple direction, then two, and then three. For example, for three directions, say, "Please pick up the book, put it on the table, and come sit by me." If all three are followed in the proper order, you'll know your child can remember three directions. Identify her limit and wait until she's older before giving her more complicated directions.

Let Your Young Child Do as Many Things by Herself as Possible

Because she wants to march to the beat of her own drum and have total control over her own life, your young child will fight for the chance to make choices. Whenever possible, give her the opportunity to develop her decision-making skills and increase her self-confidence. The more control she feels that she has, the less likely she'll be to reject taking directions from someone else.

Avoid Unnecessary Rules

Analyze a rule's importance before you etch it in stone. Your young child needs as much freedom as possible to develop her independence.

SOLVING THE PROBLEM

What to Do

Give Simple, Clear Directions

To make it easier for your child to follow your directions, be as specific as possible about what you want your child to do. Make suggestions but don't criticize what she's done. For example, say, "Please pick up your toys now and put them in the box," rather than, "Why don't you ever remember to pick up your toys and put them away on your own?"

Praise Following Directions

Reward your child for following your directions by praising her job well done. You are also showing her how to appreciate someone's effort by saying "Thank you for picking up all of the markers off of the floor." This role-modeling praise teaches her to express gratitude to others.

Play Beat-the-Clock

Set the timer on your smartphone for one minute. Then tell your child "Let's see if you can start picking up your toys before the timer on my phone sounds! Ready, set, go!" This "game" motivates her to leave her fun for something you want her to do.

Praise Your Child's Progress

Be a cheerleader as your child takes steps toward completing your requested task. For example, say, "That's great, the way you're getting up and starting to put those toys away."

Use Grandma's Rule

Children are more likely to follow directions when they know they can do what they want to do after a task is completed. For example, say, "When you've picked up the books, I'll push you on the swing," or, "When you've washed your hands, we will have lunch."

Practice Following Directions

If your child is not following your directions, find out whether she's unable or unwilling by walking her through the task. Guide her manually and praise her progress along the way. If you discover she can do the task but simply refuses to, say, "I'm sorry you aren't following directions. Now we have to practice." Practice five times. Then give her the opportunity to follow the directions on her own.

If she still refuses, say, "It looks like we need more practice. When you finish practicing, then you may play with your toys."

What Not to Do

Don't Back Down if Your Child Resists

Say to yourself, "I know my child doesn't want to do what I want her to do, but I'm more experienced and know what's best for her. I need to teach her by giving her clear directions so she can eventually do things herself."

Don't Punish Your Child for Not Following Directions

Teaching your child how to do something, instead of punishing her for not doing it, avoids your becoming a source of stress in her life and helps her learn how to follow directions.

CASE HISTORY: "DO WHAT YOU'RE TOLD!"

Four-and-a-half-year-old Evan Jackson knew his alphabet and his numbers, and he was even starting to sound out words in his favorite books. The one thing he couldn't do was the one thing his mother wanted most: follow her directions. On a daily basis, Evan's mother would give him simple directions such as "Evan, please pick up your toys and then put your dirty clothes in the basket," or "Come sit here on the couch and put on your boots." Evan would get about halfway through the first task, and then he'd lose track of what he was supposed to be doing and wander off to investigate a toy truck or see what his brother was doing.

"How many times do I have to tell you what to do?" his frustrated mother would yell. "You never listen to me! You never understand what I tell you!"

This continued until one day Evan shouted back, "I can't do all those things!"

His mother actually "heard" what he said and took it seriously. She decided to try limiting her directions to one simple command, to see if Evan could do that. "Evan, please bring me your boots," she asked simply. Evan marched right over to his blue-and-white boots and brought them to his mother, who clapped her hands with delight. "Thanks so much for doing what I asked!" she said. A while later, she asked Evan to go get his coat on. When Evan fulfilled her request, she again followed up with praise for his effort.

Evan's mother learned that it was better to teach her son to follow her directions by limiting the number of requests she made of him, rather than threatening and screaming at him. She realized that listening to Evan's feelings was crucial to their positive relationship. She slowly increased the number of directions she gave her son, waiting until he was able to do two at a time before giving him three at a time. Her clear language and use of Grandma's Rule helped her win the war against Evan's not following directions.

Overeating

DEFINING THE PROBLEM

The appetite of many young children can be as boundless as that of the famous Cookie Monster on *Sesame Street.* Like the puppet hero, your child may not be aware of why he wants more food than he needs. Because overeating is a symptom of a problem, not the problem itself, try to discover the reasons behind your child's seemingly bottomless pit of a stomach. Possible explanations include habit, emotional comfort, boredom, mimicry, or the desire for attention. Help him find ways to satisfy his needs and wants without overeating. However, get professional help if your child is a consistent overeater. Avoid putting a child on a diet that is not medically supervised.

PREVENTING THE PROBLEM

Model a Healthy Attitude toward Food

Your relationship with food is contagious. When you complain about dieting or being too fat, for example, your child learns that food has power beyond being enjoyable and making him healthy. Food becomes the enemy to defend against, lest he lose control and pig out on a forbidden chocolate cake.

Since moderation is the key to health, moderate your talk as well as your behavior. Eating disorders in young children have become much more prevalent, due in part to our dieting-obsessed and body image-obsessed culture.

Become Informed about the Amount of Food That Is Appropriate for Your Child

Consult your child's healthcare provider for answers to specific nutrition questions about your child. For more information about recommended guidelines for young children, consult the website Choosemyplate.gov.

Serve Healthy Foods

Keep junk food out of your overeater's reach so he won't be tempted to choose it. And don't use junk food as a bribe or a reward!

Check Your Child's Diet

Since your young child is too young to know what he should and shouldn't eat, it's up to you to establish healthy eating habits – the earlier the better. Learn more at the website Choosemyplate.gov.

Teach When, How, and Where Eating Is Allowed

Restrict eating to the kitchen and dining room only. Slow down the pace of eating and insist that food be eaten from a plate or bowl, instead of directly from the refrigerator. Taking more time between mouthfuls allows our brains to get the message that we're full before we've eaten more than we need. This process takes about 20 minutes.

SOLVING THE PROBLEM

What to Do

Provide Pleasurable Activities Other Than Eating

Get to know what your child likes to do besides eat. Suggest these activities after he's eaten enough and after enough time has passed for his brain to let him know that he's not hungry anymore.

Provide Nutritious Between-Meal Snacks

A well-timed snack can prevent your child from getting overly hungry and gorging at mealtime when it finally arrives.

Watch When Your Child Overeats

Try to discover why your child overeats by seeing if he turns to food when he's bored, mad, sad, watching others eat, or wanting attention from you. Help him resolve his feelings by talking or playing, instead of using food.

Control Your Own Eating Habits

If parents snack on empty-calorie junk foods all day, their children will be inclined to do the same.

Praise Wise Food Selections

You can mold your child's food preferences by your tone of voice and by encouraging him to eat foods that you want him to favor. Whenever your child picks up an orange, for example, say, "That's a great choice you made for a snack. I'm glad you're taking care of yourself so well by eating yummy treats like oranges."

Encourage Exercise

Overweight children often don't eat any more than normal-weight children; they just don't burn off enough calories through exercise.

If you live in a cold climate, suggest physical activities to do inside in the winter, like dancing or jumping rope. In the summer, try activities such as swimming, walking, baseball, soccer, and swinging. All these are not only good for your child's physical development, but they also relieve tension, give him fresh air, and build his coordination and strength. Your participation will make exercise even more fun for your child.

Give Your Child Positive Attention

Praise his artwork, the clothes he's chosen, the way he's cleaned up his toys, and so on to give him positive attention for things that are not food related.

What Not to Do

Don't Reward with Food

Don't offer food as a present or reward. This helps you avoid teaching your child that eating means more than satisfying hunger.

Don't Give In to His Desire to Overeat

Your child may keep asking for another hot dog, for example, after he's eaten two. Use common sense about quantities of foods that you give your child to consume at a sitting. This is your job as a caring, supportive, protective parent.

But just because your child wants more food doesn't mean he should have it at that moment. Satisfying his hunger is important, so say, "I think two hot dogs are enough for now. Let's play for a few minutes and then we can talk about having another hot dog, if you want to." In this way, you are teaching him to recognize what is an appropriate amount of a certain food while showing respect for his desires and wishes.

Don't Give Treats When Your Child Is Upset

Your child may begin to associate food with emotional (rather than physical) nourishment if you consistently offer treats to comfort him when he's upset.

Don't Consistently Allow Food While You're Watching TV

Avoid teaching your child to associate food with TV. It's a good idea to limit his television viewing time for many reasons (see Too Much Screen Time, page 262), including because television advertising bombards your child with food-related messages. If possible, record his favorite shows and zip through the commercials.

Don't Give Junk Foods as Snacks

What you allow for snacks and meals is what your child will expect. Food preferences are learned, not inborn.

Don't Make Fun of Your Child If He Overeats and If He's Overweight

Calling him a name, such as "Chubby," doesn't solve the problem of overeating. It does create another problem, however: it becomes his identity so he thinks that chubby is who he is rather than the result of his eating too much food, eating too quickly, and eating unhealthy food.

CASE HISTORY: "NO MORE COOKIES!"

Three-year-old Olivia Hanlon was getting a reputation at preschool and family functions for being a "walking bottomless pit." If food was in sight, Olivia ate it. She never seemed to be full.

"No, you can't have another cookie, Olivia!" Eva Hanlon would scream every time she caught her daughter with her hand in the cookie jar. "You've had enough cookies to last your lifetime!" But neither angry outbursts nor the threat of taking away her tricycle lessened Olivia's desire to finish every morsel in a box or on a plate. Eva decided to consult her pediatrician to learn how to change Olivia's eating habits. The doctor provided a nutrition plan and recipe suggestions specifically tailored for Olivia. The doctor also explained that when children eat very fast, as Eva had said Olivia did, their brains don't tell them they are full until later.

The next day, Olivia wolfed down the suggested amount of oatmeal and asked for another helping, but Eva finally had an answer that wasn't angry or insulting: "I'm glad you liked the oatmeal, Olivia. We can have some more tomorrow morning. Let's go read that new book now." Eva knew that the amount that she had given Olivia was nutritionally adequate and that her stomach would eventually send her brain the message that it was full. This made it easier for Eva to stand firm when Olivia begged for more oatmeal. It was also easier for Eva to plan each meal, because she knew what amounts were enough to nourish her daughter.

At meals, Olivia's parents engaged her in conversation and praised her when she slowed her frantic eating pace. They also ended their steady supply of cookies, so Olivia started to try new foods that were tasty and more nutritious. Eva praised Olivia's choices every time she chose a healthy food, saying "That's great that you picked carrot sticks for a snack."

Overusing "No!"

DEFINING THE PROBLEM

No ranks as the most-likely-to-be-used word among toddlers. This is because it's the most-likely-to-be-used word among parents, who use it to exercise power and control over their little ones when they are behaving inappropriately. Toddlers are famous for getting into, on top of, and underneath things that they shouldn't, and parents are famous for saying "No! Don't touch!" or "No! Don't open!" or "No! Don't do that!" or just "No, no, no!" In addition, little ones learn quickly that *their* saying no can be a powerful tool to get their own power and control over what they want when they want it.

PREVENTING THE PROBLEM

Get to Know Your Child's Personality

If you're familiar with your child's needs and wants, you'll know when her "No!" means no and when it really means yes or something else. In other words, don't always take her literally when she says no to every request.

Limit Questions with Yes-or-No Answers

Avoid questions your child can answer with "No." For example, ask her how much juice she wants, not whether she wants some. If you want her to get in the car, don't say, "Do you want to get in the car?" Say, "We're getting in the car now," and then do it!

Change Your "No!" to Something Else

The best way to reduce the frequency of your toddler's use of *no* is by limiting the number of times she hears you say no, as well as by limiting her opportunities to use it as an answer. For example, use the word *stop* instead of *no* when your child is doing something that you don't want her to do.

Redirect Your Child's Behavior

Because you usually want your child to stop a behavior when you say no to her, teach another behavior to replace the one you want stopped. For example, if your toddler is digging in the potted plant, instead of saying no, simply say, "Please stop digging in the plant. Let's play with the dollhouse instead." This redirection moves her to a new behavior and avoids the use of the dreaded *no.*

SOLVING THE PROBLEM

What to Do

Ignore Your Child's "No!"

If you're not sure what she means by no, assume she really means yes. For example, if she doesn't want the juice she just said no to, she won't take it. Eventually, you'll know when she really means no.

Let Your Child Say No

Even though she must still do what you want (or need) her to do, your child is entitled to say no. When you want her to do something but she has said no, explain the situation to her. For example, say, "I know you don't want to pick up your crayons. When you've picked up the crayons, then you may play with the markers." This lets your child know that you've heard what she's said and are taking her feelings into consideration – but you still want her to do what you've asked.

What Not to Do

Don't Laugh or Encourage the Use of No

Laughing or calling attention to your child's overuse of the word *no* only encourages her to use it more to get your reaction.

Don't Get Angry

Remember that the "'no' stage" is normal in your developing toddler and will soon pass. Getting angry will be giving your child attention for saying no, and attention and power are just what she wants.

CASE STUDY: NEGATIVE NATHAN

20-month-old Nathan Shelby's favorite word to say was his parents' least favorite word to hear: *no.* Because little Nate used that word to answer every question asked of him, his parents started to wonder about his mental powers. "Can't you say anything besides no?" they'd ask their son, only to get his usual response.

So the Shelbys tried to reduce the number of times that they used the word during the day, to see if that would have an effect on Nathan's vocabulary. Instead of saying "No, not now," whenever Nate demanded a cookie, they'd say, "Yes, you may have a cookie when you've eaten your dinner." And while they were still, in effect, saying no, Nate didn't react negatively in return. Instead, he took his parents up on their promise and got his cookie immediately after dinner.

As his parents traded in their *no's* for *yes's,* Nate started to increase his use of *yes,* a word that was immediately met with smiles, hugs, and compliments from his delighted parents. "Thanks for saying yes when I asked you if you wanted to take a bath," his mother would say. They were delighted that their son was decreasing his *no's* in direct proportion to how much praise he got for saying yes.

The Shelbys also tried to limit the number of questions with yes-or-no answers they asked Nate. Instead of asking him if he wanted something to drink with his dinner, they asked, "Do you want apple juice or milk?" Nate would happily make a choice between the two. Their efforts were painless ways to manage their son's negativity, and they soon found their household taking on a more positive tone.

Plane Travel Stress

DEFINING THE PROBLEM

Flying with young children to visit grandparents or just for family vacation can lead to high parental anxiety. How do you keep a restless, active young child corralled in the small space of an airplane seat for all that time? The excitement of the airplane and all the people can overload a young child to the point of crying and open rebellion at having to sit strapped in for what seems like an eternity.

And even before the flight, there's the necessary child-related equipment that must be carried along with the whining, squirming little bundle. You are allowed to take your child's car seat on board, but make sure you learn your airline's rules for the age limit on free travel. For example, ask the airline how old your little one needs to be before he must have his own ticket or boarding pass. And managing security, the waiting area, the boarding lines, and the storage of carryon bags before the flight can be overwhelming. But if fly you must, then managing the menagerie is your task to accomplish in the caring ways listed below.

PREVENTING THE PROBLEM

Employ Entertainment Central

Keeping little minds occupied in close quarters requires a lot of entertainment. So grab as many fun travel-friendly items as possible, such as books, small toys, little puzzles, tablet computers, etc.

Practice Before Traveling

If this will be your child's first trip, it's good to first practice everything you'll do on the way to Grandma's house. Your dining chairs can become airplane seats, doorways can be metal detectors, and kitchen counters can become X-ray conveyers. Walking through the boarding routine and seating will at least partially prepare your child for what lies in store.

Make Travel Rules

Simple rules, such as those you have for any outing, will establish boundaries of behavior. So give your child rules like these: stay close, listen to instructions, hold my hand, keep your seatbelt buckled, and spend no more than ten minutes on the tablet computer.

Get Your Child His Own Luggage

Children love to imitate adults, so a wheeled carryon bag with toys and games inside can let your child feel like a fellow traveler. It will push him to exhibit more grownup behavior to match how he's feeling.

Use Your Car Seat

Airlines recommend taking your child's car seat on board as an extra safety measure. Not only is it safer, but it is also familiar to your child and more comfortable for him than sitting low in an airplane seat with a lap belt. He will be more likely to stay buckled in because that's the rule you have in your car.

Take the "Red Eye"
If possible, schedule a flight at night so your child can sleep during most of it. Again, a car seat can help because it will probably be more comfortable for sleeping.

SOLVING THE PROBLEM

What to Do

Use Empathy
At the first sign of rebellion, stop what you are doing and begin talking calmly to your child. Say, "I understand you don't want to sit any longer, but that's the rule. The pilot will tell us when we can get up. I know you can wait. You are being so patient."

Walk It Off
Tour the waiting area to keep from sitting too long before the flight. During the flight, walk the aisle if you can to keep little legs busy.

Offer Activity Rewards
When your child gets restless, offer a fun activity that you have kept stored for such an occasion. Say, "I know you are tired of sitting, so when you have read another of your books, you may play on the tablet computer for 15 minutes. I know the game you like is fun, too."

Use Praise
Keep complimenting your child's good behavior throughout the trip. Say, "You are sitting so quietly," or, "Thank you for playing with your puzzle box."

What Not to Do

Don't Lose Your Cool

Your child will sense your mood, so keep telling yourself "This is okay. I can handle this. This is no big deal." This affirmative self-talk can reduce your anxiety and won't panic your child.

Don't Offer Food Rewards

When your child gets restless on the plane or while awaiting its departure, don't use food as an incentive for him to follow the airplane "rules." Using food as a reward can make food overly important and lead to inappropriate behavior, just to get a desired treat. Instead of food, use Grandma's Rule to motivate your child and use activities as a reward. Say, "When you sit down in your seat, you and I can sing softly to each other!"

Don't Threaten

Making threats only creates a response in your child that can be toxic, as he will worry about being on the receiving end of your anger. Saying such things as "If you don't behave, we'll just go home," won't teach him appropriate behavior, even if you are willing to give up your flight tickets. In addition, you will become the source of your child's stress, not of caring and support. Using praise and activity as rewards keeps your behavior caring and encouraging for your child.

If your child starts crying and won't stop, or if he throws a tantrum while on an airplane flight, see Temper Tantrums, page 224.

CASE HISTORY: TRAVEL TROUBLE

Emma was a bright and energetic two-and-a-half-year-old, and her grandparents wanted very much to see her. So they gave her mother, Ellie, tickets for a flight to their retirement home in the warm, sunny South. Although Ellie wanted to see her parents and spend a week in a warm place after the fierce winter they had suffered through, she was worried about taking Emma on a plane trip. And she would have to do it alone because her husband, Wyatt, couldn't get off work to go with them.

Ellie worried about the trip for a whole week but then decided to accept the offer. "What's the worst that could happen during a three-hour flight?" she asked Wyatt. To find out what it might be like to travel with a young child, Ellie and Wyatt began asking their friends about their experiences, and the answers they got didn't put them at ease. They heard stories of out-of-control children, screaming adults, cranky passengers, and lost favorite toys. Ellie was about to back out of the trip until she said to herself, "I've handled worse than what I've heard about traveling with kids. I can handle this trip."

Ellie and Wyatt began planning what Emma would need to keep her happy on the flight. Ellie borrowed the cutest carryon bag from her friend, and Emma wheeled it around the house for days, filled with things she wanted to take to "Bama and Papa's." Every day, Ellie and Emma would set up chairs in a row and pretend to be flying.

When the day to fly came, Wyatt took his precious cargo to the airport for their flight. Emma was cooperative and followed the rules that they had made about getting through security and into the waiting area. Wheeling her carryon, Emma and Ellie explored the terminal. Finally, they boarded. Ellie buckled Emma's car seat into the airplane seat, and Emma climbed in. During the flight, Ellie began handing out new toys, books, and games as Emma requested them or got tired of the one she had. By the time they arrived at their destination, Emma had napped and was fresh and ready for her visit. Ellie was also relaxed after a good trip. The worst that had happened throughout the whole time was what Elite's wild imagination had conjured up: a week's worth of worry before the trip even started!

Refusing Help

DEFINING THE PROBLEM

"Me do it!" is one of the lines parents of young children can expect to hear starting around a child's second birthday. This declaration of independence provides a golden opportunity for parents to allow their young try-it-alls to perfect their skills, as long as they don't break household rules. So dig deep for extra patience as you bear with your child's mistakes, and balance the need to get chores done against the importance of teaching your little one important skills of independence.

PREVENTING THE PROBLEM

Assume Your Child Can Do It for Himself

Keep track of your child's changing levels of expertise. Make sure you've given him a chance to try something before helping him or doing it for him so you don't underestimate his current ability.

Buy Clothing Your Child Can Manage

Buy clothes that easily go up and down for your child in potty training, for example. Buy shirts that will go over his head and not get stuck on his shoulders when he puts them on. Avoid tedious buttons.

Store Clothing in Coordinated, Accessible Units

Help your child develop an eye for coordination by sorting his clothes. Make them accessible by putting them in bins or drawers that he can easily reach.

Prevent Frustration

Try to make tasks as easy for your child to accomplish as possible. Undo the snaps on his pants or start the zipper on his coat, for example, before you let him finish the job.

SOLVING THE PROBLEM

What to Do

Play Beat-the-Clock

Tell your child how much time you have for a certain activity. Doing so will help him understand that it's not his inability to do something that makes you take over the job if you have to move more quickly than he does. Set your phone timer for the number of minutes you want to allow for the task and say, "Let's see if you can get dressed before the timer sounds." This also helps your child learn a sense of being on time, and it reduces the power struggle between you and your child. You're not telling him to do something – the timer is.

Suggest Cooperation and Sharing

Because your child doesn't understand why he can't do something and doesn't realize that he'll be able to do it eventually, suggest sharing the job by having him do what he can while you do the rest. For example, when putting shoes on a one-year-old, say, "Why don't you hold your sock while I put on your shoe." Whenever possible, let your child accomplish some portion of the task instead of merely watching you and feeling inadequate.

Make Effort Count

As your child's first and most important teacher, you can encourage him to attempt various tasks. Say, for example, "I like the way you put on your T-shirt. That was a great try. Now, I'll help you turn it around so the picture's in the front."

Remain as Calm and Patient as You Can

If your child wants to do everything – saying "I'll put on my shorts," or "I'll open the door," or "Me close the drawer" – then remember that he's asserting his independence, not his obstinacy. Since you want him to learn to do things by himself, let him try. Avoid getting upset when he doesn't do things as quickly or precisely as you'd like. Instead, take delight in the fact that your child is taking the first step toward being self-sufficient and be proud of him for taking the initiative.

Allow as Much Independence as Possible

Let your child do as much by himself as he can so frustration doesn't replace his innate curiosity. While putting on his shoes, for example, don't insist on keeping his other shoe away from his fidgety fingers if he wants to hold it. He can hand it to you when you're finished with the first.

Ask Your Child to Do Things – Don't Demand

To make your young child more likely to ask for things nicely, show him how to make requests politely. Say, "When you ask me nicely, then you may play with the blocks." Then explain what you mean by *nicely*. For example, teach your child to say, "Please, may I get a fork?" when he wants a fork.

What Not to Do

Don't Punish Your Child's Mistakes

There are bound to be a few mishaps along the way, so be patient. If your child tries to pour the milk himself and accidentally spills it, help him pour it more carefully the next time. Don't expect success right away.

Don't Criticize Your Child's Efforts

Avoid pointing out your child's mistakes. If he puts his sock on inside out, simply say, "Let's put the smooth side of the sock inside, next to your foot, okay?"

Don't Feel Rejected

Don't feel hurt because your child doesn't appreciate your help. He's trying to do things on his own, and he may perceive your help as an obstacle. If he says, "Let me open the door," let him do it. He knows you can do things faster and with less effort, but he wants and needs to develop his skills. Appreciate his efforts to do things on his own.

CASE HISTORY: INDEPENDENT ISABELLE

During the first three years of Isabelle Manning's life, her mother, Sarah, did everything for her. But then suddenly, "Miss Independence" wanted her mother to do nothing for her – a personality change that was confusing and frustrating for Sarah Manning. "I can't stand waiting for you, Isabelle! You're not old enough to do that by yourself," Sarah would say when they were late for preschool and Isabelle would insist on putting her coat on by herself.

The waves of demanding and refusing to comply began to subside when Sarah realized that the problem was causing her to dislike

Isabelle's desire to do things herself. One morning while Isabelle was dressing to go to school, Sarah noticed Isabelle putting on her coat for the first time. "That's great, the way you put on your coat," Sarah said. "You're really hurrying to get ready for school! I'm so proud of you!" Isabelle let her mother finish the zipper without putting up a fight, something that hadn't happened in weeks.

As they rode to school, Sarah realized how independent her daughter was becoming. Sarah continued to praise her daughter's efforts at achieving independence. She also made it as easy as possible for Isabelle to complete her tasks, and Sarah and Isabelle began to work together to finish jobs when necessary.

Sharing Struggles

DEFINING THE PROBLEM

Mine! is the buzzword young children use to remind each other (and adults) of their territorial rights. Despite the wars this four-letter word incites, children's possessiveness will unfortunately not disappear until children are developmentally ready to share. Help lay the groundwork for peace by consistently teaching your young one the give-and-take rules of the world. Enforce these sharing rules at home, but be patient. Don't expect them to be righteously followed until your child starts sharing without your intervention – that's the glorious sign that she's ready to broaden her boundaries.

PREVENTING THE PROBLEM

Make Sure Some Toys Belong Strictly to Your Child

Before young children can let go of the word *mine* and all the things attached to it, they must be given the chance to possess things. Put away your child's favorite toys or blankets when visitors come over to play so she won't be forced to share them.

Point Out How Your Friends and You Share

Show your child that she isn't the only one in the world who's expected to share her things. Give examples at neutral (non-sharing) times of how you and your friends share things. Say, "Marie borrowed my scissors today," or, "Charlie borrowed my lawnmower."

Point Out What Sharing Means and How Much You Like It

Tell your child how nicely she's sharing whenever she's allowing another person to hold or play with her toys. For example, say, "I like the way you're sharing by letting your friend hold the blocks."

Put Labels on Similar Toys (for Twins or Children Close in Age)

Make sure you don't confuse your daughter's teddy bear with her sister's or brother's. Label each one with a nametag or piece of thread to help your child feel confident in her ownership.

Set Up Sharing Rules

Before friends come over to play, let your child know what's expected of her at group sharing times. For example, say, "If you put a toy down, anyone may play with it. If you have it in your hands, you may keep it."

Understand That Your Child May Share Better at a Friend's House

Because toys and other items your child encounters away from home are not exclusively hers, she may be less possessive about them when she's not defending her own territory.

Remember That Sharing Is a Developmental Task
Learning to share is an accomplishment that cannot be rushed.

SOLVING THE PROBLEM

What to Do

Supervise Your Child's Play
Stay close and pay attention while your child is playing with others. This will help you resolve sharing conflicts that she's too young to handle without you.

Set the Timer
When two children are calling a toy "Mine!" show how the give-and-take of sharing works. Tell one child that you'll be setting the timer on your smartphone and that when the timer sounds, the other child may have the toy. Keep using the timer until they've grown tired of the toy.

Take Toys to Calm Time
If a toy is creating a problem because one child won't share it, put the toy in calm time to remove it from the situation. If the toy is out of reach, it can't cause any trouble. Say, "This toy is causing a problem. I will take it to calm time." If the children keep fighting over the toy after it's been brought back, keep removing it to make the point that not sharing a toy means no one gets to play with it.

What Not to Do

Don't Get Upset
Remember that your child will learn the rule about sharing when she's developmentally ready, not when you force her to do so. When you see your child sharing, you'll know she's ready!

Don't Punish for Not Sharing

If your child has trouble sharing, remove the offending toy rather than punishing your child. This puts the blame on the toy, not the child.

CASE HISTORY: LEARNING TO SHARE

Three-year-old Liam Smith knew what the word *sharing* meant: it meant that he couldn't sit and hold as many toys as he wanted when his friend, Jason, came over to play.

"You must share!" Liam's mother told her son after another day of Liam's clutching his toys and saying "Mine!" whenever his mother said, "Now, Liam, let's share." Then one day, Nora Smith screamed, "If you don't share, I'm going to give all of your toys to poor children who will appreciate them," and Liam tearfully gave up his toys.

That night, after Liam was tucked in bed, Nora told her husband "Liam just doesn't know how to share." This simple statement shed new light on the problem. The Smiths realized that they needed to teach Liam what sharing really meant. So the next time Liam's cousins came over, Nora took him aside for a talk. "Liam, here's the new sharing rule: Anyone can play with anything in this house as long as another person is not holding it. If you or Mike or Alexis is holding a toy, no one can take it away. Each of you may play with only one toy at a time." Nora also told Liam that he could put away one favorite toy, which could belong to him and him alone.

The next few hours were tense for Nora, but Liam seemed to be more relaxed. He began by holding only one toy and letting his cousins have their pick of the lot in the toy box. "I'm so proud of you for sharing," his watchful mother praised him as she oversaw the operation. But when she ventured off to fix lunch, the familiar "Mine!" cry brought her back to the playroom. The new "burp-itself" doll was being pulled limb from limb by Alexis and Liam. "This toy is causing trouble," Nora stated matter-of-factly. "I will take it to calm time."

The children stared in disbelief as they watched poor Burping Betsy sitting in the calm time chair, looking as lonely as a puppy that had been put outside for misbehaving. After two minutes, Nora returned the toy to the children, who had long since forgotten about it and were busy playing with interlocking blocks.

As the weeks went by, the children played side by side, with the toys spending fewer minutes in calm time to restore peace. This was particularly due to the fact that Liam was more open to letting "his" toys be "their" toys during the play period.

Shy Behavior

DEFINING THE PROBLEM

Imagine seeing your neighbor, Kathy, at the supermarket as you're happily shopping with your three-year-old daughter, Samira. Suddenly, Samira clutches your leg and won't answer Kathy's simple greeting of "How are you, Samira?" You're surprised at Samira's sudden shyness and ask her "What's the problem? You love Kathy!"

Children's "freezing up" when greeted by adults confuses many parents. While some children approach the world with unbridled curiosity, others keep tight rein on their inquisitiveness, choosing to look before they leap. Both tendencies are considered normal, each reflecting an innate style. In other words, shyness is not a problem in and of itself. However, a child's shyness becomes a problem when it becomes so powerful that it prevents her from making friends or participating in social activities away from home, such as going to a birthday party or the library. Teaching social skills and role-playing various social situations will help young children reduce their shyness and increase their self-confidence.

PREVENTING THE PROBLEM

Develop Realistic Expectations and Goals

How you expect your child to act around other people may not be realistic, given her developmental stage and temperament. For example, if your two-year-old isn't ready to go to a birthday party, forcing her to go will only create more fear about future social events. Young children overcome their shyness as they gain experience interacting with others. However, don't expect changes overnight.

Accept Your Child's Shyness

Children are born with different temperaments. Some are friendly and outgoing, some are cautious and shy, and some bounce back and forth between the two. Instead of sending your shy child the message that something's wrong with her because she doesn't act according to your expectations, accept her shyness as part of her unique temperament.

Compliment Your Child

When your child makes a comment during a conversation, pay her a compliment. For example, say, "I like what you said about the puppy, Samira. He does have an unusual white paw."

Be a Good Role Model

Give your child plenty of opportunities to watch you interact with people in social situations. Also, role-play different scenarios with your child, teaching her what to say in certain situations. For example, say, "When people ask me how I feel, I usually say, 'Fine. How are you?'"

SOLVING THE PROBLEM

What to Do

Use Understanding and Empathy

When your child seems to be shy in social situations, say, "I understand how you feel. Sometimes I don't want to meet others." It's important to understand that although you may say to yourself, "My child MUST come down to Thanksgiving Dinner!" or, "It's awful that my daughter is so shy," overreacting and exaggerating the situation in this way reinforces the behavior because it gives her power and recognition for her position as the shy one. When she is ready to join the group, she will do so. Welcome her with open arms!

Practice Responding to Questions

If your child shifts into shy mode, she's probably telling you that she may need to learn how to answer questions. Practice with her while you're riding in the car or playing in the bathtub. For example, say, "When somebody says, 'What's your name?' say, 'Samira.' That way, they'll know who you are. Now, let's practice. When I ask what's your name, what do you say?" Practice with her several times each day until "Samira" is the automatic response.

Practice with Family and Friends

Provide your child with opportunities to participate in conversations. For example, say, "What do you think about having pizza for dinner tonight?" or, "Tell your dad about your trip to the zoo today." If you have more than one child, take turns participating in conversations by calling each child by name and asking specific questions of each child.

Seek Professional Help if Necessary

If shyness is interfering with your child's happiness and is keeping her from participating in appropriate activities, seek help from a qualified professional.

What Not to Do

Don't Humiliate or Shame

Even though you may say to yourself, "I am so embarrassed by my child's shyness," shaming or blaming her by telling her that she's ruined Thanksgiving or humiliating her by telling her "Don't be so silly!" will not help her be more comfortable in social situations. Instead, it will further discourage her from becoming socially confident.

Don't Apologize

Apologizing for her behavior by telling others that she's your shy child or that she doesn't speak will only deepen her fear of others.

Don't Beg

Although you may be sorely tempted to beg your child to answer the nice lady, doing so will give her reticence considerable power and will encourage more refusals in the future.

Don't Label

Making excuses to family and friends by saying your child is shy creates a self-fulfilling prophecy she has to live up to. It also discourages her from trying to behave differently in the future.

CASE HISTORY: GETTING TO KNOW GABRIEL

Gabe Bartone was a shy baby who would turn his face away from strangers or bury his head in his mother's shoulder when strangers were around. His dad, Michael, had also been shy as a child. Gabe's Grandma Leona said that no one outside the family heard Michael talk until he was almost a teenager!

Gabe's mother, Maria, had hoped that Gabe would outgrow his shyness. But at five years old, Timid Gabe, as she called him, showed no signs of becoming more outgoing. Michael understood his son and the pain that he felt when he was confronted with talking to strangers. So Michael worked out a plan to help his son. First, he engaged him in conversation by asking lots of questions that required more than a yes-or-no answer. Michael asked, "What did you have for lunch today?" or, "What games did you play at school today?" When Gabe answered with more than one or two words, Michael would say, "Gabe, I'm glad you told me about that," or, "That was a really interesting story about playing airplane on the playground."

Michael and Gabe also practiced greeting people. The two would pretend that they were meeting on the street, and Gabe would say, "Hello, how are you?" Michael would answer, "Fine, thank you. And you?" Then they would both laugh.

Eventually, Gabe began to relax more around people he didn't know well, and family and friends started to comment on how polite he was becoming. Gabe's mom and dad were happy for him. They had expected him to follow Michael's timid path, and they were thrilled to see him coming out of his shell. They pledged to each other that they would never again put a label on their son.

Sibling Rivalry

DEFINING THE PROBLEM

Tattling on brothers and sisters and hating a new sibling from the first day he invades the family are just two examples of how sibling rivalry wreaks havoc on family relationships. Because young children are constantly flapping their wings of independence and importance, they often fight with their siblings for space, time, and the number one position in their most important world: their family.

But even though sibling rivalry is part of human nature, showing each of your children that he or she is special can decrease sibling rivalry's frequency. To keep sibling rivalry to a manageable minimum, tell your children you appreciate it when they get along well together. Make sure they understand your job is to take good care of each child and be there for them when they need you.

PREVENTING THE PROBLEM

Prepare Your Child Before the New Baby Arrives

Discuss with your first child (if she's over a year old) how she'll be included in the life of the new baby. Tell her what the new family routine will be and how she'll be able to help out. This will help her understand that she's an important part of loving and caring for her younger brother.

Play with Your Older Child Whether Your Baby Is Asleep or Awake

To decrease the sibling rivalry associated with a new baby, make sure you play with your older child when your new baby is awake, as well as when he's asleep. This will prevent your older child from concluding that you only give her attention when the baby's out of sight. Spending time with your older child no matter what the baby is doing makes your older child think, "I get Mom's attention when the baby's here as well as when he's gone. That baby's not so bad after all!"

Make Realistic Getting-Along Goals

Don't expect your child to smother the new baby with as much tenderness as you do. She may be older than the baby, but she still needs lots of individual attention.

Plan Time Alone with Each of Your Children

Even if you have half a dozen young children to attend to, try to plan time alone with each of them (a bath, a walk, or a trip to the grocery store). This will help focus your attention on each child's needs, and it will keep you informed about feelings and problems that may not surface amid the roar of the crowd at home. Make individual brag boards (for twins or children close in age). Display each child's creativity in her own special place to reassure each child that her efforts merit individual attention.

SOLVING THE PROBLEM

What to Do

Let a Timer Manage Children's Taking Turns

When your children are fighting for your undivided attention, let your smartphone timer determine each child's turn. This teaches your children about sharing, and it lets each child know that he or she will have a turn being your number one object of attention.

Offer Alternatives to Fighting

Allowing fighting to flare up and burn out of control doesn't teach your children how to get along. Instead of allowing battles to be fought, give your children a choice: they can either get along and have fun or not get along and lose fun time. Say, "You may either get along with each other and continue to play or not get along and be separated in your calm time space to think about getting along." Let them get in the habit of making choices to give them a feeling of control over their lives and to help them learn to make good decisions on their own.

Define "Getting Along"

Be specific when praising your children for playing nicely together so they know what you mean when you say they're getting along. Say, "That's great, the way you're sharing and playing together so nicely. I really like how you're getting along so well. It makes playing together fun."

What Not to Do

Don't Respond to Tattling

Children tattle on each other as a way of enhancing their position with their parents. Stop this game of one-upmanship by saying "I'm sorry you aren't getting along," and by pretending that the tattling didn't occur. Even if a dangerous activity has been reported, you can stop the activity and still ignore the tattling.

Don't Set Up One Child to Tattle on Another

Asking your older son to come tell you when his baby sister is doing something wrong is not a good way to teach your children how to get along without tattling. Besides, you (or another person on your parenting team) need to be close by to supervise your children's play.

Don't Get Upset When Your Children Don't Love Each Other All the Time

Children cannot live in the same home without engaging in some rivalry. It's human nature. Keep friction to a minimum by rewarding getting along and by not allowing the rivalry to escalate to fighting.

Don't Hold Grudges

After the dispute has been settled, don't remind your children that they used to be enemies. Start over with a clean slate and help them do the same.

CASE HISTORY: STARR WARS

The constant warfare between five-year-old Jason Starr and his three-year-old sister, Julie, made their parents wonder why they'd ever had children! Feeling overwhelmed by the noise, decision making, and constant need to support their children, the Starrs jokingly complained to each other that their kids obviously didn't appreciate the sacrifices that they had made to buy them nice clothes, new toys, and good food. It seemed as if all that Jason wanted to do was tease and pinch his sister. These were his favorite ways of letting his sister have it when he thought she was taking up too much of his parents' time and attention. Threats of punishment obviously weren't working to solve the problem, since Jason didn't seem to mind getting yelled at whenever he started bullying his sister.

The only time Grace Starr ever noticed her son being nice to his sister was when he helped her across an icy patch on the driveway. Grace was so grateful for the bit of decency that she told her son, "That's great, the way you helped your sister be safe. I'm really proud of you." The Starrs decided to encourage more acts of kindness by dishing out compliments when their children got along and by enforcing a new rule when their children began to fight. They got the chance to put their new policy into practice later that day when a battle over books broke out after they got home from the library. Grace had no idea who'd started the argument, but she told her children "You have a choice now, kids. Since I don't know who took the book from whom, you can get along like you did in the car today or you can be separated in calm time."

Both children ignored Grace's mandate and continued to play tug-of-war with the books. So she followed through with her promise, saying "You've both chosen to spend some time in calm time. Julie and Jason screamed their way through most of their calm time, but after quieting down and being allowed to get up from their chairs, they had different looks on their faces for the rest of the day. They began to act like comrades rather than enemies, and Grace was delighted that she had not lost her temper when her children had.

The Starrs continued to praise getting along. They put less emphasis on any fighting they noticed, and they consistently used calm time to separate the children and reinforce the consequences of the children's choosing to fight.

Stealing

DEFINING THE PROBLEM

Since everything in the world belongs to a young child until someone tells her differently, it's never too early to teach her not to take things from others unless you approve of it. So every time your child takes things that aren't hers, enforce consequences that will help her develop a sense of right and wrong.

PREVENTING THE PROBLEM

Make Rules

To encourage your child to let you know when she wants something, teach her how to ask for it. Decide what may and may not be taken from public places and others' homes and let your child know your expectations before you go out. A basic rule might be "You must always ask me if you can have something before you pick it up."

SOLVING THE PROBLEM

What to Do

Explain How to Get Things without Stealing

Your child doesn't understand why she can't take things when she wants them. Make her aware of correct and incorrect behavior by saying "You must ask me for a piece of gum before picking up the pack at the grocery store. If I say yes, you may pick it up and hold it until we pay for it."

Explain What Stealing Means

Make sure your child understands the difference between borrowing and stealing (and the results of each), to make sure that she knows what you mean when you say, "You must not steal." Stealing is taking something without permission; borrowing is asking for and getting permission before taking something and then giving it back.

Make Children Return Stolen Objects

Teach your child that she cannot keep something she's stolen. Enforce the rule that she must return it herself (with your help, if necessary).

Have Your Child Pay for Stealing

To help her realize the cost of stealing, have your child work off the theft by doing odd jobs around the house or by giving up one of her prized possessions. Say, "I'm sorry you took something that didn't belong to you. Because you did that, you must give up something that does belong to you." The possession she gives up could be returned to her several months later as a reward for good behavior.

Enforce Calm Time

When your child takes something that doesn't belong to her, let her know that she must be isolated from people and activities because she broke the rule. Say, "I'm sorry you took something that wasn't yours. I am taking you to calm time."

What Not to Do

Don't Be a Historian

Don't remind your child about a stealing incident. Bringing up the past will only remind her of wrong behavior and won't teach her how to avoid the mistake in the future.

Don't Label Your Child

Don't call your child a thief because she will eventually behave according to how she's labeled.

Don't Ask Your Child Whether She's Stolen Something

Asking only encourages lying. She'll say to herself, "I know Mommy will be mad. Why not lie to avoid her feeling bad?"

Don't Hesitate to Search Your Child

If you suspect that your child has stolen something, verify it by searching her. If you discover that she did steal, make sure to enforce the consequences. For example, say, "I'm sorry you took something that didn't belong to you. Now you must pay for it by giving up one of your belongings and returning what you stole."

CASE HISTORY: THE SHORT SHOPLIFTER

Sandy and Doug Berk had never broken the law and gone to jail, and they didn't want their four-year-old son, Logan, to do so either. But they worried that if he continued to steal gum, candy, toys, and other objects that caught his fancy while shopping with his parents, he might not have a future outside of prison.

"Don't you know that stealing is wrong?" Sandy would scream at her son when she'd catch him red-handed. She also tried slapping his hand and telling him he was a bad boy, but that didn't do any good, either. She became afraid to go on errands with her son, dreading both the embarrassment of his behavior and how she would feel when she punished him.

Logan was totally oblivious to the reasons why stealing was forbidden. He didn't understand why it wasn't fine to take things that didn't belong to him. So the Berks decided to explain the situation in terms he could understand. "Logan, you cannot take things that you do not pay for," Doug began. "You must ask me for a pack of gum. If I say yes, you may pick up the pack and hold it until we pay for it. Let's practice."

Logan was delighted to oblige because now when he asked for gum, as the rule stated, his mother and father complimented him for following the rules and they paid for the gum. But the Berks didn't always say yes to Logan's request. So when Logan tried to get away with taking a candy bar without first asking his mother to pay for it, Sandy enforced her second rule by making him lose a privilege of playing with his toy candy bar – his favorite pretend toy. "Because you took this candy bar," she told her son as they walked back into the store, "you will have to give up your toy one when we get home and give this real candy bar back to the store." Despite Logan's protests, Sandy did take away his beloved toy. "To earn the toy back," she explained, "you have to follow the rules by asking first and by not taking what is not paid for."

After several weeks of praising Logan for following the rules, Sandy gave him his toy candy bar back, and both parents began to feel more secure about their frisky little son's future.

Stranger Safety

DEFINING THE PROBLEM

"Don't talk to strangers," is an admonition millions of parents dish out to their young ones. The warning is valid, but this subject deserves more attention that just a one-sentence admonition. Everyone who is on the parenting team needs to reinforce this message from a child's earliest mobile years: Children need to learn how to behave with strangers when you are there with them, just as they need to learn how to interact with family, friends, and acquaintances. In addition, they need to learn what to do when strangers approach them when you are not there with them.

When you're with your child, minimize her fear of strangers by teaching her how to be friendly to people she doesn't know. At the same time, teach her what to do when approached by a stranger when you're not there. Both you and your child will feel more secure knowing that she understands what to do when you're there and when you're not.

When you are at the park or playground, remember: eyes on your child, not on your phone or another screen! Children under the age of eight may not spend the majority of their time without adult supervision. But they still need to learn this lesson about how to interact, or not interact, with strangers.

PREVENTING THE PROBLEM

Establish the Rules

Let your child know your rules about interacting with strangers. A basic rule could be "When I'm with you, you may be friendly and talk to people you don't know yet. But when I'm not with you, don't talk to or approach anyone you don't know – that person is a stranger. If a stranger asks you to go with him and tries to give you anything, yell as loudly as you can 'NO! GET AWAY FROM ME!' Then run to the nearest house, ring the doorbell, and tell the person there what happened."

Practice Following the Rules

Pretend you're a stranger and ask your child to follow your rules concerning strangers. Rehearse several different scenarios, making sure she knows how you want her to respond.

Don't Frighten Your Child

Instilling fear of strangers only breeds confusion and doesn't teach your child what to do. She needs to know how to think on her feet when strangers invade her privacy. Being fearful will destroy her ability to behave rationally.

Teach About Who You Consider a Stranger

Stranger is a strange word for young children, so define a stranger as a person your child has not yet met. A stranger can seem to be a really nice person, but if your child doesn't know him or her, then the "Don't talk, run," rule applies.

SOLVING THE PROBLEM

WHAT TO DO

Remind Your Child of the Rule by Praising Correct Behavior

If your child says hello to a stranger while you're present, show your approval by saying "I'm so glad you're being friendly. Now tell me the rule about behaving with strangers when I'm not with you." Then praise your child's remembering the rule.

Encourage Your Child to Be Friendly

Friendly children tend to be more readily accepted by others as they go through life, so teaching friendliness is important. However, it's also important to explain to younger and older children how to be friendly and keep themselves safe. For example, suggesting that your child say hello to strangers when you're with her encourages her to be friendly. But not allowing her to say anything to strangers when you're not with her helps keeps her safe.

Set Stranger Boundaries

It's impossible for children to quickly distinguish between potentially dangerous strangers and ones who are harmless. That's why you have to establish a rule about how to interact with strangers when you're not present. Explain to your child that being friendly with strangers, whether you're there or not, never includes taking offers of candy, gifts, rides, or helping them find lost pets. (Also see Protect Your Child Against Victimization, page 20)

WHAT NOT TO DO

Don't Instill Fear of People

To help your child avoid the danger of being molested, teach her your rules about dealing with strangers. However, don't teach her to fear people. Fear only inhibits correct decision making, regardless of age.

Don't Worry about Your Child's Bothering Others by Being Friendly

Even if strangers don't acknowledge the greeting, it's good for your child to learn how to offer one at appropriate times (i.e., when you are with her).

CASE HISTORY: KEEPING CADEN SAFE

"How can we teach our five-and-a-half-year-old son to be friendly yet keep him safe when we're not around?" This was the challenge Leah and Ian Docking faced in trying to solve the problem of their very friendly son, Caden. They explained to Caden who a stranger was and then said the rule, "Do not talk to strangers when we are not with you."

Caden followed their orders so intently that he became terrified of strangers and began to throw tantrums every time his parents took him to the shopping center or grocery store. He didn't want to see strangers, he explained to his mother, because they were so mean and dangerous that he couldn't even say hello to them. The Dockings were frustrated to see their well-intentioned instructions backfire this way. They finally realized that Caden didn't understand the difference between saying hello to strangers when they were with him, which they wanted to encourage, and saying hello to strangers when they were not with him, or going with strangers, or taking things from them – which they wanted to prevent. Caden didn't understand because the Dockings had not given him the chance to understand.

Leah told her son, "The new rule is that you can talk to anyone you want when I'm with you. But if I'm not with you and someone offers you something or wants you to go somewhere with him, ignore the person, start yelling as loudly as you can, and run as fast as you can away from the person who approached you. Go to the nearest house or nearest adult in a store and tell them what happened."

The Dockings practiced this rule at home by role-playing with Caden. They pretended that they were in a shopping center, his mother was the stranger, and his dad was the adult in the store that Caden could go to when the stranger came up to him and offered him candy. Caden soon became comfortable with the rule, after going through the process safely at home. Leah reminded her son of the rule on a weekly basis, until it became a habit for him. To reinforce the lesson, Leah practiced saying hello to others, too, when she and Caden were together. Caden noticed this and praised his mom's actions, just as she had praised his following the rule.

The Dockings' concern for Caden's safety never completely disappeared. So from time to time, they asked Caden to practice stranger safety as he grew into elementary school, to convince themselves that he understood and remembered this potentially life-saving behavior.

Talking Back

DEFINING THE PROBLEM

When backtalk (sarcasm, sassy retorts, and unkind remarks) spews forth from your young child's previously angelic mouth, you become painfully aware of her ability to mimic words (good and bad) and control her world with them. As with other forms of language, backtalk can only be learned by exposure to it. So limit your child's opportunities to hear unpleasant words by limiting her access to electronic media that use them.

PREVENTING THE PROBLEM

Talk to Your Child the Way You Want Her to Talk to You

Teach your child how to use the well-mannered language you want to hear. Say, "Thank you," "Please," "I'm sorry," and other polite phrases. Have your child practice using the words you've modeled. Remember that young children are the world's greatest imitators.

Decide What Constitutes Backtalk

In order to react fairly to your child's increasingly diversified verbal behavior, you need to determine whether your child is talking back or doing something else. For example, sarcasm, name-calling, shouting answers, and defiant refusals all constitute backtalk. Simple refusals like "I don't want to," may be simple statements of fact. Questions such as "Do I have to?" are expressions of opinion. Make sure your child understands what *you* mean by backtalk.

Monitor Friends, Media, and Your Own Speech

Limit your child's exposure to backtalk by keeping tabs on what words slip through your lips. Also monitor friends, peers, family members, and television characters. What goes in young children's ears comes out of their mouth.

SOLVING THE PROBLEM

What to Do

Wear Out the Word

Overusing a word reduces its power. Therefore, help your child grow tired of using an offensive word by having her repeat it for one minute for each year of her age. Say, "I'm sorry you said that word. I'll set the timer. You must say the word until the timer rings. When it rings, you can stop saying the word." After the word is worn out, she'll be less likely to use it in the heat of the moment.

Ignore the Backtalk

Try to pay as little attention to inoffensive backtalk as you can. Pretending the event didn't occur takes away the backtalker's power over you. The game isn't much fun to play without the anticipated payoff of your reaction.

Compliment Nice Talk

Let your child know what kind of talk you prefer by praising her for using desirable language. Say, "I like it when you answer me kindly when I ask you a question, just as we practiced. That makes me feel good."

Use Politeness and Respect for All

Be polite and respectful to your child, as if she were a guest in your home. Your politeness will show her how to be polite, and your respectful manner will tell her that she is with a caring adult.

What Not to Do

Don't Play a Power Game

Since you know that using backtalk is one way your child tries to get power over you, don't use backtalk yourself. She may find fun ways of entertaining herself by seeing how she can get you mad or get your attention by using backtalk. You don't want to encourage that.

Don't Teach Backtalk

Sarcastically or angrily shouting answers back at your child, or anyone else, only shows her how to use backtalk. Although it's hard not to yell when you're being yelled at, teach your child how to be respectful by being respectful to her.

Don't Punish Backtalk

Backtalk is, at worst, annoying. No evidence supports the belief that we make children respectful by punishing them for disrespect. Only fear is taught through punishment.

CASE HISTORY: OLIVER'S BACKTALK

Whenever Ava Martinez would ask her four-year-old son, Oliver, to do anything, Oliver would shout, "No! I don't like you! I'm not going to!" Oliver became so experienced at backtalk and verbal abuse that whenever he was asked any kind of question, he would angrily shout back his answer, as if he had forgotten how to answer someone politely.

"No child of mine is going to talk like that!" Dominic Martinez, Oliver's father, would shout back at his son.

Unfortunately, Dom's backtalk would cause an even greater uproar in the family. Once they realized that their sarcasm and shouting were teaching their son this kind of behavior, they tried hard to react calmly to Oliver's backtalk and to praise his pleasant responses. So one day, they asked Oliver to put his toys back in his toy box. When he calmly said, "Okay," they responded by saying, "That's really great, the way you answered so pleasantly by saying okay."

It wasn't hard for the Martinezes to control their anger. As Oliver's yelling and sassy talk became less frequent, they usually pretended they didn't hear it. The combination of setting a consistently polite and respectful model for Oliver and praising his in-kind responses ended the outbreak of backtalk and helped create a much more pleasant and cooperative household.

Temper Tantrums

DEFINING THE PROBLEM

Millions of normal, lovable young children throw temper tantrums as their way of coping with frustration or anger or to tell the world they're the boss. Tantrums can become less frequent and even be prevented by not giving the performer an audience and by not giving in to his demands.

Though you may want to give in or crawl under the nearest checkout counter when your child throws a tantrum in public, be patient until he's finished and praise his gaining control after he's calm. Being there for him when he needs support after a tantrum assures him that he has a caring adult in his corner, no matter what.

Note: Common, periodic crying is not a temper tantrum and needs to be treated differently. Get professional help if your child has more than two to three temper tantrums per day.

PREVENTING THE PROBLEM

Teach Your Child How to Handle Frustration and Anger

Show your child how adults like you can find other ways of coping besides yelling and screaming. If you drop your smartphone and see the cracked glass, instead of yelling and throwing your own tantrum, say, "I'm upset now, honey, but I can handle it. I'm going to try to be more careful with my things." Regardless of the situation, teach your child to look at the choices he has to solve his problems, instead of getting violent about them; at the same time, model care for possessions.

Praise Coping

Catch your child acting good. For example, praise his asking you to help him put together a complicated puzzle that might otherwise frustrate him. Say, "I'm so glad you asked for my help instead of getting mad at the puzzle." Helping your child handle his frustration and anger calmly helps him feel good about his ability to cope with problems. You'll find him repeating a problem-solving technique when he knows he'll get praised for it. Say, "I'm really proud of you for being able to solve the problem calmly."

Use Empathy

After a tantrum, hold your child and tell him that you understand his frustration. Say, "I know how you feel when things get tough, and I'm here to help you solve a problem when you need me."

Don't Let Playtime Always Mean Alone Time

Be there and pay attention to your child when he's playing appropriately with his toys. When you do, he won't have to resort to inappropriate play or tantrums to get your attention.

Don't Wait for an Invitation

If you spot trouble brewing with your child, don't let it simmer too long. When you see that the situation is difficult or frustrating for him, say, "Let's do it this way." Show him what to do and then let him complete the task. This will help him understand that it's good to let others help him when he needs help.

SOLVING THE PROBLEM

What to Do

Ignore Your Child's Tantrum

Do nothing for, with, or to your child during his performance. Teach him that a temper tantrum is not the way to get your attention or get his demands met. But how do you ignore a tornado tearing through your living room? Walk away from him during his tantrum, turn your back on him, put him in his room, or isolate yourself. If he's being destructive or dangerous to himself or others in public, put him in a confined place where he's safe (but not in a dark closet). Don't even look his way during this isolation. Though it's tough to turn away, try to busy yourself in another room of the house or with another activity in public.

Try to Stand Firm

Despite the power of your child's screaming and pounding, make sure you maintain self-control by holding tight to your rule. Tell yourself silently that it's important for your child to learn that he can't have everything he wants when he wants it. Your child is learning to be realistic, and you're learning to be consistent and to give him boundaries for acceptable and unacceptable behavior.

Remain as Calm as You Can

Say to yourself, "This is not a big deal. If I can stay in control of myself, I can better teach my child to control himself. He's just trying to pressure me so he can have what he wants." Keeping calm while ignoring his tantrum is the best model for him when he's upset.

Praise Your Child

After the fire of a temper tantrum is reduced to smoldering ashes, immediately praise your child for regaining self-control. Then get both of you involved in a favorite game or activity that isn't frustrating for him or you. Say, "I'm glad you're feeling better now. I love you, but I don't like screaming or yelling." Since this is your only reference to the tantrum, it will help him know that it was the tantrum you were ignoring, not him.

Explain Rule Changes

If you and your child are at the store and he asks you to buy a toy that was off-limits before, you can change your mind – but you should change your message, too. Say, "Remember when we were here before and you threw a tantrum? Since you're behaving nicely now by staying close to me, I've decided that you can have the toy." This will help him understand that it wasn't the tantrum that changed your mind; it's that you're buying the toy for another reason. If you like, tell him why you've changed your mind, particularly if in doing so you praise him for his good behavior.

What Not to Do

Don't Reason or Explain During the Tantrum

Trying to reason your child out of his tantrum during the tantrum is wasted breath. He doesn't care. He's in the middle of a show and he's the star. Any discussion at this time only encourages the tantrum because it gives him the audience he wants.

Don't Give In to the Tantrum

When your child throws a tantrum and you give in and get him what he wants just to calm him down, you are teaching him to throw a tantrum to get what he wants. When you say no, mean it! Giving in only tells him you aren't as good as your word.

Don't Throw a Tantrum Yourself

Say to yourself, "Why do I need to act crazy? I know that when I said no, I said it for a reason." Losing your cool only encourages your child to keep the heat on, and it shows him that he doesn't need to learn self-control.

Don't Belittle or Shame Your Child

Just because your child has a temper tantrum doesn't mean he's a bad person. Don't say, "Bad boy! You are such a baby! Aren't you ashamed of yourself?" Your child will lose respect for himself and feel that he didn't deserve what he wanted anyway. Belittling is just another form of bullying.

Don't Be a Historian

Don't remind your child of his tantrum later that day. This only gives more attention to the behavior and increases the chances of his having another tantrum, just to be the center of your conversation.

Don't Make Your Child Pay for the Tantrum

Continuing to ignore him after it's over will only cause him to have more tantrums to try to get your attention back. Don't send him the message that he's unloved and unwanted just because his behavior was.

CASE HISTORY: TANTRUM TIME

Gavin and Kaitlyn MacLean were worried about their two-year-old daughter, Madison, who would get a bad attack of "temper tantrumitis" every time her request for a cookie before dinner was refused. When her parents said no, she would scream "Yes!" pull on her father's pant leg, jump up and down on the kitchen floor, and then throw herself down and kick and scream until both she and her distraught parents were exhausted. That's when Gavin and Kaitlyn would finally give in.

In frustration, the MacLeans wondered what they were doing wrong. Was there something terribly wrong with saying no to Madison's demands? It finally occurred to them that Madison's tantrums were more frequent when they said no to her. They also realized that giving in to Madison's uncontrollable desire for a cookie before dinner only encouraged her bad behavior.

The next time Madison had a tantrum, they were ready with a new strategy. Instead of saying no, Kaitlyn said matter-of-factly, "Madison, I know you want a cookie. You can have one when you're quiet and have finished your dinner."

Madison didn't stop her tantrum, so her parents simply walked away, leaving her with no audience for her big scene. Although it was hard to stay away from their screaming child, the MacLeans waited until their daughter was quiet before entering the kitchen. Without any physical or verbal attention, Madison had eventually stopped wailing and was waiting to see if her parents would practice what they preached.

Her father appeared, wearing a smile, and said, "Madison, I know you want that cookie now. When you've eaten your dinner and we're ready for dessert, then you may have the cookie. I'm glad you're not screaming and yelling now. It's nice to see you controlling yourself." To her parents delight, Madison did quietly eat her dinner; so as promised, she received her cookie when she was finished eating.

The MacLeans complimented themselves later that night on the self-control that they had exhibited in not giving in to Madison's tantrum. Although they were tempted later on to give in, they continued to remove themselves from their daughter when she had a tantrum and praised her anytime she reacted calmly when something was denied her. The frequency of Madison's tantrums diminished, and while she would cry from time to time when she was disappointed, she wouldn't have the explosive scenes she'd often had in the past.

Testing Limits

DEFINING THE PROBLEM

Immersed in new discovery and pushing their way out into the world, young children who have just discovered crawling or walking may need to be pulled back to safety because they're not as self-sufficient, self-reliant, and self-controlled as they think. As your little one grows, let him go only as far as you know is safe. Get to know your child's limits by testing his maturity and responsibility before making the mistake of allowing him more freedom than he can safely handle. Allow him freedoms that are commensurate with his abilities and give him frequent opportunities to reinforce your belief that he's mature enough to handle those freedoms. Also remember that, on average, boys test their limits and demand freedom sooner than do girls.

It's good to let young children exercise their curiosity and explore their world – with your guidance and protection. Also see Exploring Off-Limits, page 112; and Appendix II: Childproofing Checklist, page 288 for making your house safe before your child starts to roam the range!

PREVENTING THE PROBLEM

Establish Limits and Communicate Them Clearly

Your child needs to know his limits before he can be expected to do what you want him to do. If you decide that the dining room is off-limits to your toddler, teach him how he can go into that room safely – meaning only with you. And make sure that you or another adult is around to help him practice following this rule. Making a space in your home forbidden territory only makes it more of an attraction.

Childproofing Is Smart-Proofing

Always lock the doors to cabinets holding household cleaners and other dangerous items. (See Appendix II: Childproofing Checklist, page 288)

Let Your Child Know When He Can Cross the Boundaries

Reduce the attraction of certain no-no's by showing and telling your young adventurer how he can do what he wants without getting in trouble for it. For example, say, "You must hold my hand while you cross the street," or, "Mommy goes with you when we play on the porch."

Ask About the Rules

Before you let your older child play outside, ask him about the rules you have set for outside play. If he doesn't remember, restate the rules.

SOLVING THE PROBLEM

What to Do

Offer Rewards for Staying within Limits

Encourage your child to stay within the limits by rewarding him for doing so. Say, "I'm happy you stayed at the swing set. Now you may swing for three more minutes." Of course, make sure that a responsible adult is watching him play, to ensure that he is safe and to share in the positive relationship building that doing so provides.

Be There

Because a toddler or preschooler is discovering his world with unbridled curiosity, he needs to know what is safe and what isn't – and you or another adult needs to be watchful about what he does. For example, if your little one is walking around the house testing out his new mobility, be there beside him to guide him and prevent him from getting into dangerous situations. He may pick up the window screen handle and try to throw it at the glass pane, or he may open/close the wooden shutters only to get his little fingers stuck in them! All of these things and more can happen in a moment while your head is turned! Let him explore, but teach him what is and isn't okay, with a watchful eye on his comings and goings.

Establish Consequences for Not Respecting Limits

Teach your child that not heeding your limits brings his fun to a stop. Say, "I'm sorry you knocked down the gate to the dining room. Now let's practice what to do when you come to the gate." Be a watchful eye reinforcing his practicing going up to but not knocking down the gate, saying "I like the way you looked over the gate at all of the things in the dining room. Looking at all of the pretty colors and shapes is so much fun!"

Be Consistent

Make sure you enforce the rules every time your child breaks one. This teaches him you mean what you say. It also helps him feel more secure about his actions when he's away from you, because he'll clearly know what you expect him to do.

Use Frequent Praise

While watching your child explore or play outside, take time out to praise his following the rules. For example, say, "Good staying in the yard," or, "You are being so careful as you climb."

What Not to Do

Don't Spank Your Child for Going into the Street

Spanking doesn't prevent your child from doing something again – it just encourages your child to hide from you the next time he does what you punished him for. Children who sneak into the street are in great danger, of course, so don't add to the problem by making them want to do it on the sly.

Don't Overreact When You See Your Child Pushing Limits

When you panic and yell about danger, your child senses your stress, which increases his stress level. However, he doesn't understand that your stress is connected to the danger you perceive. Stay calm and remove him from the danger while explaining why you were concerned.

CASE HISTORY: ASHLEY ON HER OWN

Six-year-old Ashley Hamilton was the most popular little girl on Twelfth Street, a situation that also caused her behavior to be the biggest problem in the Hamilton family. At breakfast one morning,

Ashley told her mother "Today, I'm going to walk to school with Susie, then I'm going to Donna's house after lunch, and then I'm going to play dolls with Maria." When her mother told Ashley she couldn't go anywhere anytime she pleased, Ashley shouted, "Why? Why not? I'm going anyway! You can't stop me!"

These kinds of rebellious statements encouraged angry name-calling episodes between Ashley and her parents, who couldn't decide where freedom should be given and boundaries should be drawn to protect their "baby" from dangers she wasn't old enough to handle. Because Ashley was constantly getting invitations, the Hamiltons couldn't ignore the problem of choosing where and when she could go. So they decided to establish rules that could be changed depending on how Ashley managed her freedom and responsibility. The Hamiltons clearly explained these rules to Ashley, who was more than happy to learn how to get more freedom. And because Ashley was learning to read, they decided to write the rules on a big chart Ashley could see every day.

One of the things Ashley needed to learn was which rules to follow when she spent the night with her best friend. Her parents knew her best friend's parents and called them to discuss the rules that they had at their house. When the Hamiltons were satisfied that Ashley could manage her friend's house rules, they gave her permission to go there. And before she went, the Hamiltons reminded Ashley about the good-manners rules that they had at home. They did this to help Ashley's taste of freedom be as sweet as it could be. Establishing and practicing the conditions of freedom allowed everyone to feel safe, secure, and satisfied within the limits and expectations provided.

Toilet-Training Accidents

DEFINING THE PROBLEM

Toilet training is the first major battle of wills between parents and young children. The war breaks out when parents ask their independence-loving offspring to give up doing something that has been natural for them to do. Instead, parents want their children to begin doing something that is new and often undesirable.

To most children, what is desirable about toilet training is pleasing their parents. So foster the least accident-prone toilet training possible by putting more attention on what your child should do (keep his pants dry, go potty in the potty) than on what he shouldn't do (go potty in his pants). Help your child feel proud of himself while you lessen the likelihood that he will have an accident just to get your attention and reaction.

Note: If your child is having continuous toilet-training accidents after the age of four, consult a medical professional. This chapter does not discuss bed-wetting because many preschoolers are simply not developmentally able to stay dry all night. Many bed-wetting experts believe that after age six, bed-wetting may be considered a problem that requires professional help.

PREVENTING THE PROBLEM

Look for Signs of Toilet-Training Readiness (Usually Around Two Years of Age)

The generally accepted signs of readiness include a child's awareness of the fact that he's urinating or having a bowel movement (or is about to do so), more regular and predictable elimination patterns, the ability to pull his pants down and climb on the toilet or potty chair (and do the opposite), the ability to understand toilet training terminology and follow simple directions, an interest in using the toilet, and a general dislike of having a soiled diaper.

Don't Train Too Early

Early training simply teaches children to depend more on their parents than on their own ability to manage using the toilet. Children who are forced to learn before they're ready may take longer to master using the toilet.

Model Correct Potty Behavior

Familiarize your child with the potty and how it's used by showing him how you go to the bathroom (and how he can when he's ready).

Make It as Convenient as Possible for Your Child to Use the Potty When He Needs to Go

Keep the potty chair in the kitchen or another convenient place, for easier cleanup after accidents during toilet training. Take the potty with you in the early stages, to help your child feel comfortable about using the potty outside your home.

Choose a Toilet Training Procedure and Stick with It

Many resources (books, tapes, videos, and websites) are available to help you toilet train your child. Find one that feels comfortable to you and consistently follow through with the methods it recommends. For example, go to http://mayoclinic.org/ healthy-lifestyle/infant- and-toddler-health/indepth/potty-training/art-20045230/ Consistency and patience are the keys to success!

SOLVING THE PROBLEM

What to Do

Reward Being Dry as Well as the Correct Use of the Toilet

Teach your child to keep himself dry by telling him how good staying dry is. This increases his awareness of what you want him to do (stay dry) while wearing training pants. While your child is in training pants, say to him about every 15 minutes, "Check your pants. Are they dry?" This gives him the responsibility of checking his dryness, which makes him feel more in control of the process. If he's dry, tell him you're glad. Say, "How nice that you're staying dry."

Remind Your Child of the Rule for Going Potty in the Wrong Places

Many young children occasionally go to the bathroom in an inappropriate place (outside, for example). When your child does this, remind him that the rule is "You're supposed to potty in the potty. Let's practice." Then proceed with practicing correct pottying procedures.

React Calmly to Accidents

If your child is wet, say, "I'm sorry that you're wet. Now we need to practice staying dry." Then practice ten times going to the toilet from various parts of the house. (Pants down, sit on the toilet, pants up. Then repeat these steps from the next part of the house.) In practice, it's not necessary for your child to urinate or have a bowel movement – just to go through the correct motions for using the toilet.

Use Grandma's Rule in Public

When your child wants to go only in his potty when you're in a public place, try Grandma's Rule. Say, "We need to keep dry. We can't use your potty because it's not here. When you've used this potty, we can stay here at the zoo." If you prefer, take your child's potty with you.

What Not to Do

Don't Punish Toilet-Training Accidents

Punishment only gives your child attention for going potty in his pants (or another wrong place). It doesn't teach him how to stay dry.

Don't Ask the Wrong Question

Saying "Check your pants," increases your child's awareness of what you want and puts him in charge. It's a good substitute for "Do you need to go potty?" which is generally answered with a no. Help your child feel responsible for checking his dry-wet condition and doing something about it.

Don't Shame

Don't try to get your young child to stay dry by saying "Shame on you! You are too old to have accidents." This will only make him hide accidents from you, and it won't teach him how to stay dry.

CASE HISTORY: KAYLEE'S "ACCIDENTS"

As soon as preschool let out for the summer, nearly four-year-old Kaylee Winter started to lose more than her knowledge of numbers and letters. Her occasional toilet training accidents signaled that she was waiting too long before heading for the bathroom. Kaylee had discovered that she could relieve the physical pressure of having to go by releasing only a small amount of urine into her pants. When her mother would scold her for wetting her pants, Kaylee would point out how she had wet "just a little." Claire realized that Kaylee was just too preoccupied with her activities to take time out to run to the bathroom, and to her, just a little wet was no big deal.

After analyzing the situation, Mike and Claire Winter decided to reinstate the routine they had used to toilet train their daughter the previous year. They once again began praising Kaylee's dry pants instead of getting upset when she had wet ones. "Check your pants, Kaylee. Are they dry?" Claire said the next morning after breakfast. She was delighted when Kaylee happily said yes with a big grin.

"Thanks for keeping yourself dry, honey," Claire then said, giving her daughter a hug at the same time. "Let's keep them dry all day!"

After a few days of periodically asking Kaylee to check her pants (Kaylee always found herself dry), Claire thought her problem was behind her – until the very next day, when Kaylee was wet again. "It looks like you've forgotten how to go potty. Let's practice ten times going to the potty," she told her glum-looking daughter, who seemed very disappointed that she now had to spend her valuable playtime practicing. Kaylee also missed her mother's praise when her pants were dry. But Kaylee soon learned that it was easier to go to the potty and get the praise for dry pants than it was to practice ten times when her pants were wet.

Kaylee continued to follow through with keeping her pants dry for several months. For the rest of the year, the Winters occasionally praised Kaylee for staying dry, as a reminder. Instead of becoming angry and frustrated when their daughter was wet, they kept in mind that it was better to help Kaylee firmly reestablish a love of dry pants.

Too Much Screen Time

DEFINING THE PROBLEM

Young children are growing up in a world flooded with an ever-expanding variety of electronic media – including TV, computers, tablets, smartphones, and video games. These media can become addictive because of the fast-paced, emotionally charged images that they produce.

Although your little one may be quiet and happy while engaged in screen time, research has demonstrated the danger of letting him become addicted to watching screens instead of having screen time as only one of his activities. In addition to screen time, your child needs active play outside to build his healthy mind and body and prevent obesity; time to read a book to help him create images in his mind, based on words he's reading; and creative play with non-electronic toys to build his gross motor and fine-motor skills.

A child's brain develops rapidly during his first years, and young children learn social skills by interacting with people, not screens. Rather than the stimulation of screen time, what young children really need is face time with a caring adult. Studies have also shown that excessive media use can lead to attention problems, school difficulties, sleep and eating disorders, aggressiveness, and obesity. In addition, media can provide platforms for illicit and risky behaviors.

PREVENTING THE PROBLEM

Limit Screen Time

Neuroscience research demonstrates that very young children learn best during "talk time", one person communicating with another. Passive video presentations do not lead to language learning in infants and young toddlers According to the American Academy of Pediatrics, optimal educational media opportunities begin after age two, when media may play a role in bridging the learning achievement gap. However, it is vitally important for all children to spend time in outdoor play, reading, hobbies, and using their imaginations in free play, as well as in developing language through interacting with other children and adults.

Establish Screen-Free Zones

Make sure there are no TVs, computers, or video games in children's bedrooms or in eating areas, and make sure that you and your children do not use phones or tablets in restaurants or while eating at home. This is an easy way to reduce the temptation to be online and on-screen all the time, so it automatically reduces the risk of your child becoming addicted to screens.

Go Screen-Free When You Are Interacting with Your Child

When you are playing, diapering, feeding, bathing, or simply talking with your young child, turn off the TV, put away your smartphone, and power down your tablet. He doesn't need the distraction of electronics while you and he are having fun together! (See Section Two, page 9)

Stand Your Ground

When your child sees that his favorite screen is not on, demands you turn it on, and throws tantrums when you don't turn it on, stick to your rules about how much screen time is healthy for a child of a certain age and maintain the screen-free zones that you have established. Giving in whenever he demands screen time does not teach him frustration tolerance, the ability to delay gratification, or the importance of following rules.

Become Your Child's Companion

When you make yourself available to your child for one-on-one time, he will want less time with electronics. Children love having the undivided attention of a caring adult!

SOLVING THE PROBLEM

What to Do

Cultivate Creativity

Instead of letting your young child become a passive media sponge, focus his attention on building forts, inventing games, drawing pictures, creating collages, and doing other creative activities to keep his growing mind and body active.

Redirect His Attention

When your young child has a temper tantrum because you turn off his favorite screen or because you won't give him your cell phone or electronic tablet to play with, you know that screens can be addictive! Say, "I'm sorry that we cannot have screen time right now. Let's read a book!"

Monitor Your Child's Media Choices

It is vitally important when you allow your child access to screens that you participate in viewing with him. Being there and discussing what he is doing or seeing helps with language development and critical thinking. Making statements such as "I wonder why Clifford feels happy now," will help him understand the feelings he is witnessing and will help him begin to see cause-and-effect relationships. For example, when a little boy is being teased by another child, it's important for you to point out that teasing another person hurts that person.

Restate the Rule

When your child demands access to electronic media, restate the rule. Say, "Remember the rule: we can play with the phone only after naptime."

Use Grandma's Rule

When your child wants to use your smartphone or watch TV, raise the cost to him by using Grandma's Rule. Say, "When you have put the building blocks away in the box, then you may play on the tablet for five minutes."

Use a Timer

As the American Academy of Pediatrics notes, tech use, like all other activities, should have reasonable limits. Ask yourself: Does your child's technology use help or hinder participation in other activities? Set the timer on your phone to tell your child when it's time to click the off button and praise him when he turns to more physical activities. Say, "I'm glad you turned off the TV and chose to play school. What are you teaching this morning?" The quality of content is more important than the platform or time spent with media. Prioritize how your child spends his time rather than just setting a timer.

Ignore Tantrums

If your child throws himself on the floor and screams because he can't watch TV, either turn your back and wait it out or leave the room. He will eventually understand that you mean what you say.

What Not to Do

Don't Use Screens to Buy Child-Free Time

Instead of using a screen to occupy your child's time so you can be child-free in the kitchen, introduce him to the world of broiling, baking, and boiling by asking him to do age-appropriate tasks such as washing the potatoes or tearing up the lettuce.

Don't Give In

In the face of the noise of an angry child, it is tempting to just give in and let him do what he wants. Unfortunately, giving in puts him in charge and teaches him that all he has to do to get what he wants is to have a tantrum. As the caring adult in his world, it is up to you to set his boundaries, just as you do when keeping him from playing in traffic.

Keep Your Own Emotions in Check

In the face of a full-court emotional press by a child issuing you a list of demands, it is easy to lose your cool. Be a model of emotional restraint by remaining calm and telling yourself that this, too, will pass.

Don't Threaten

Telling your child that if he doesn't stop crying you will be angry or never let him watch any screen again will create stress and anxiety. Such threats erode empathy, show him you don't mean what you say, and don't teach self-regulation.

Don't Let Young Children Use Headphones

Blasting young ears with the amplified sounds from headphones can cause permanent hearing loss. Because it is impossible to monitor the volume when your young child is using headphones, it's best to just not allow their use.

CASES HISTORY: THE TV IS RUNNING THE HOUSEHOLD

From the time she got up in the morning until she went to bed at night, four-year-old Kaylee wanted screen time. While her mother, Cindy, was getting her ready to go to the babysitter, Kaylee would say, "I want to watch something!" In the car on the way to the sitter, Kaylee would also demand Cindy's smartphone and would cry and kick the back of the seat when she didn't get her way. The pattern was repeated on the way home and would continue all evening. Cindy was at her wits' end.

Cindy decided that Kaylee had been spending too much time watching TV at the sitter's and that she and her husband, Gabe, were spending too much time watching TV in the evening. So she called Natalie, the sitter, and asked how much TV Kaylee got to watch at her house. She was shocked to find out the TV was on all day. Natalee said she liked to have it on to entertain the children in her care while she diapered or fed them.

Cindy and Gabe talked that evening and decided that they would look for a new sitter or see if they could get Kaylee into some other daycare option. They had thought that using someone who cared for children in her home would provide more of a family setting and would be easier on Kaylee. But until they could find another daycare, something needed to be done at home.

First, Cindy and Gabe decided to make some rules about electronic media. The TV would be off in the morning and evening until Kaylee went to bed. Computers would be off, and cell phones would not be answered. They then planned evening activities that they could do with Kaylee.

The first few days were rough, with what seemed like constant demands from Kaylee to watch something. "I want to watch TV," she would say, and when either Cindy or Gabe answered with "I'm sorry, the rule is no TV today," Kaylee would switch to "I want to watch something on your computer." But after a few days, Kaylee shifted her attention to the play activities and seemed more content with playing with her parents. Then Cindy and Gabe reintroduced a 30-minute period of TV after dinner. Either Cindy or Gabe watched with Kaylee and talked about what was important on the program, while the other parent cleaned up after dinner. Kaylee started at a new daycare where TV was not the staple of the day, and her parents appreciated that this new parenting team member played by their rules.

Wandering Away in Public

DEFINING THE PROBLEM

Curious young children make mental lists of what to see and do at shopping centers, grocery stores, playgrounds, and so on – just like their parents do. Young children think their lists take priority, and chaos breaks out when their lists don't match their parents' lists. Your child's safety takes precedence over her curiosity in dangerous situations, so enforce your rules about public behavior despite her protests. Make staying close in public a habit for your child until you can rely on her to not do things like getting in the way of cars, pedestrians, or grocery carts. She must know what is and isn't dangerous – a distinction she must learn from you.

Note: To foster your child's staying close in public, your emphasis must be on preventing any wandering away. Once your child has left your side in public, the only thing to do is find her and prevent her from wandering away again.

PREVENTING THE PROBLEM

Use the Seat on the Shopping Cart

The seat on the shopping cart is there for the safety of toddlers, so use it to keep your wandering child restrained. Shopping cart seats also come equipped with safety belts that prevent children from standing up and getting out of the seat.

Establish Rules for Behaving in Public

Let your little one know what you expect of her in public. Say, "When we're in the store, you must stay in the shopping cart or in your stroller."

Practice Ahead of Time

If using a shopping cart seat or a stroller is not an option, then starting when your child is a toddler, practice following the rules before leaving the house. Say, "We're going to try staying within an arm's length of each other. Let's see how long you can stay close." After she does it, say, "Good staying close. Thanks for staying close to me."

Teach Your Child to Come to You

To avoid chasing your toddler through a store, teach her to come to you when you want her to. During a neutral time, take your toddler's hand and say, "Come here, please." When she comes to you, give her a hug and say, "Thank you for coming." Practice five times a day, gradually increasing the distance that your child is away from you before you say, "Come here, please." Do this until she can come to you from across the room or across the store.

Praise Staying Close

Make it worth your child's while to stay close by praising her every time she does. Say, "Good staying close," or, "You're being such a good shopper by staying close to me."

Involve Your Child in Shopping

If your child resists the stroller or shopping cart, let her hold a package or push the stroller, if she's able. This will make her feel as if she is an important part of the shopping trip, and she'll be less tempted to roam.

Change Your Rule as Your Child Changes

As your child matures and becomes able to walk away briefly and come right back to your side in a public place like a shopping center, you might change your rule and allow her to do that. Tell her why you're giving her more freedom. Knowing that she's earned more independence by engaging in safe behavior in public will help her realize that following the rules will be rewarded.

SOLVING THE PROBLEM

What to Do

Use Reprimands

Reprimanding your child for not staying close in public will teach her what behavior you expect and what will happen if she doesn't follow your rule. When you see her not staying close, say, "Please stay close. You're supposed to stay with me. Staying close to me keeps you safe." If she repeatedly breaks your rule, restate the reprimand and stop the shopping trip.

Practice, Practice, Practice

Not only is it important to practice the rules before a shopping trip, but additional practice is needed after your child has a lapse in rule following during a trip. Simply say, "I'm sorry you didn't follow the stay-close rule. Now we have to go home and practice so I know you can do it." Most children don't like to take time practicing, but it is a consequence that teaches your child what you want her to do.

What Not to Do

Don't Change Your Rules Under Pressure

Don't change your public behavior rules, even if your child yells and screams. Your being firm and consistent will give your child a sense of security. Even if your restrictions may occasionally produce yelling and screaming, the safety net you provide will help her feel protected in strange territory.

Don't Make Threats You Won't Keep

And if you know you must continue your shopping trip, don't threaten to go home if your child doesn't follow your rules. Making false promises only tells her you can't be trusted.

Don't Take Your Child Shopping for Longer Than She Can Tolerate

Some young children can follow staying-close rules for longer periods of time than others can. Get to know your child. One hour may be her limit, so consider that before leaving home.

CASES HISTORY: STAYING PUT

Emily Brody could not comfortably take her four-year-old son, Matthew, to a shopping center or grocery store anymore. He didn't want to be constrained by the shopping cart but was always wandering out of sight as soon as his mom turned her back.

"Stay here! Never run away while we're shopping!" Emily Brody screamed at her son the last time he disappeared under a lingerie rack at the department store.

Her order proved ineffective. As they left the store and strolled down the mall, Matthew ran toward a shop window, pointed upward, and screamed, "Look at that train! Look at that train!" The shop window was so far away that Emily lost sight of him for a moment, which caused her to panic.

She realized that some rules needed to be established to prevent her son from disappearing while she did her holiday shopping. The next morning, she explained the new rule to her son before they went to the grocery store. Because the grocery store was his favorite place to race from aisle to aisle, she told him "Matthew, you must stay within an arm's length of me while we're shopping. As long as you stay that close, you may look at things with your eyes, not with your hands."

During their trial run, Matthew was out of sight in minutes. "Remember the rule," Emily told him when she finally caught up with him in Aisle three and pulled him close to her. "You're supposed to stay within an arm's length of me. Staying close to me keeps you safe." Matthew acted like he didn't hear what she was saying, taking off toward his beloved granola bars. Emily, boiling inside but cool on the surface, told herself that the rules were new. Like all new rules, they'd need to be practiced before they'd be followed perfectly. "You're supposed to stay with me because staying close keeps you safe," she repeated. Then she walked him to the quiet corner by the produce and turned her back on him while staying nearby – the in-public version of calm time.

Matthew glared at his mother in protest, yelling, "No! I want to play. I don't like you!" Embarrassed but unflinching, Emily ignored his outburst. Planning her next move, she decided that if a reprimand didn't solve the problem, she'd end the shopping trip and go home to practice the shopping rules with him. Then at the end of three minutes (which seemed like three hours to Emily), she greeted Matthew with a smile and reviewed the rule as they finished shopping. Whenever Matthew stayed within arm's length, Emily praised his behavior, saying "Thanks for staying close, honey. I'm really glad we're shopping together." They then began talking about cereals and planning which ones to buy for breakfast that week.

Emily consistently reminded him of the rule over the next few weeks, but they rarely had to leave shopping and go home to practice because they were having so much fun enjoying the new closeness between them.

Whining

DEFINING THE PROBLEM

Just as adults occasionally find themselves in a bad mood for no apparent reason, young children are sometimes whiny and cranky even though their physical needs have been met. This behavior is usually the result of your child's being tired, being hungry, wanting attention, or wanting his own way. Though it may be hard to do, your ignoring the whining does help wind it down. Your child will soon learn an important rule: asking nicely speaks louder than being cranky and uncommunicative.

PREVENTING THE PROBLEM

Catch 'em Being Pleasant

When your child is not whining to ask for things, tell him how much more powerful his using a respectful, pleasant voice is. Your attention teaches him how much you appreciate being spoken to without being whined at.

Keep His Needs Met

Make sure your child eats, bathes, dresses, sleeps, and gets plenty of hugs on a regular basis, to prevent him from becoming cranky because he's wet, hungry, overtired, or too upset to tell you his feelings without whining.

SOLVING THE PROBLEM

What to Do

Define "Whining"

Make sure your child knows exactly what you mean when you say he's whining. Then explain that you'd like him to ask for something or tell you what he wants without whining. For example, say, "When you ask nicely, I'll give you the apple juice. Here's how I'd like you to ask: 'May I please have some apple juice?'" If your child isn't talking yet, show him how to indicate what he wants by using actions or gestures. Let him practice requesting things pleasantly at least five times. Make sure you fulfill his request to prove your point that asking nicely gets results.

If Necessary, Create a "Whining Place" as a Variation on Calm Time

If your child's whining continues even after you've taught him how to express his wants nicely, let him know that he has the right to have feelings and frustrations that only whining can relieve. Tell him that he can whine as much as he wants but that he must do it in the "whining place," an area designated for whining. Let him know that you'd rather not listen to whining. When he's finished whining and can tell you what he wants in a pleasant voice, he can come back. Tell him "I'm sorry you're so upset. You can go to the whining place and come back when you're feeling better."

Ignore Your Child's Whining

Because your child's whining is so nerve-racking, you can easily pay more attention to him when he's whining than when he's quiet. After you've taken him to the whining place and given him the go-ahead to get the frustration out of his system, put on headphones or do something else to help yourself ignore the whining until it's over.

Point Out Non-Whining Times

To show your child the vivid contrast between how you react when he does and doesn't whine, immediately praise his quieting down by saying "You're being so pleasant! Let's go get a toy to play with!" or "I haven't heard you whine for the longest time!" or "Thanks for not whining!"

What Not to Do

Don't Give In to the Whining

If you give your whining child attention by getting upset or giving him what he's whining for, you're teaching him that whining is the way to get what he wants.

Don't Whine Yourself

Adult complaining may sound like whining to a child. If you're doing it, your young child may think it's okay for him to do it, too. If you're in a bad mood, don't get angry with your child because you're angry with the world. Simply tell him that you're feeling out of sorts; don't whine about it.

Don't Get Angry with Your Child

Don't get angry with your child because he's having an off day. He'll not only mistake your outbursts for attention, but he'll feel a sense of power over you because his behavior created your angry response. He may continue to whine just to show you he's the boss.

Don't Punish Your Child for Whining

Responding sarcastically with "I'll give you something to really whine about," when your child whines only creates conflict between you and your child. It tells him that it's never okay to whine, which makes him feel guilty for having disgruntled feelings. As with your own behavior when you are upset, whining may be the only way your child can vent frustrations at the time.

Remember, This Won't Last Forever

Your child may be having a bad day or going through a period when nothing seems to please him, so he may spend more time whining until he gets back in sync with his world. Tell yourself "This too shall pass," while you try to lift his spirits by praising his pleasant behavior.

CASE HISTORY": THE WHINING PLACE

From the moment three-year-old Eliana Gonzalez woke up in the morning until she closed her eyes at night, she was a howling banshee of whining. Everything was said in her most whiney voice: "Mommy, I wanna eat! Mommy, what's on TV? Mommy, where are we going? Mommy, pick me up!"

Camilla Gonzalez tried to ignore her daughter's noisemaking, but she frequently gave in to Eliana's demands in order to get her to be quiet. But the whining and whimpering started to grate on Camilla's nerves until one day she screamed, "Eliana, stop that stupid whining. I'm sick of it!" But yelling at Eliana only increased her whining, so Camilla decided that to use a different method.

She decided to try a variation on using calm time, a technique that she'd used whenever her daughter had misbehaved.

"This is the whining place," she told Eliana the next morning after she began her regular whining routine. "I'm sorry you're whining now. Stay here until you're finished whining. When you're finished, get up and we'll play with your dolls."

She placed her daughter in the chair she had selected for this purpose. Then she walked away, making sure she wasn't around to give her daughter any attention. When she heard the whining stop, she returned to her daughter and praised her behavior. "Oh, I love the way you're taking in a nice voice. Let's go play."

When Camilla realized her daughter was going to the whining place nearly ten times a day, she decided to change her own behavior with her child. She began to teach Eliana how to stop herself from being taken to the whining place. "When you ask me nicely, I'll give you a drink," she explained. Then she taught Eliana how to ask nicely by modeling "Please, Mom, may I have a drink?"

Eliana practiced these instructions whenever she wanted something for which she had previously whined. Though Eliana's whining never completely disappeared (she still whined on her off days), Camilla became much happier with her relationship with her daughter. It felt very good to be a consistently caring, supportive, protective adult instead of an angry enforcer.

Appendix I

Milestones of Healthy Childhood Development

Children grow and develop according to a set, recognizable pattern. These milestones are presented below, according to the ages at which children usually reach them. Since each child develops on an individual timetable, your child may be ahead of, at, or behind the statistical average. Consult your child's healthcare professional if your child is consistently delayed in reaching milestones or if you're concerned about other aspects of his development.

Remember, girls often reach these milestones before boys do, so take that into account as you review your child's development. It is also useful to note that many behaviors that seem unique to a particular age may repeat at a later age. For you, this means your efforts to change a behavior in your three-year-old may have to be repeated when he reaches age six. But take heart. Because you were able to manage the problem effectively when he was three, it will be easier to manage it if it reemerges at six.

Birth to Three Months

- Lifts her head and turns her head from side to side, while on her tummy
- Grasps toys and holds them tight for a brief time
- Gradually responds to the sound of your voice
- Studies hands and feet and focuses on your face during feeding
- Can see at a range of 8 – 2 inches (as a newborn)
- Begins tracking objects (at two months)
- Smiles on purpose, blows bubbles, and coos when you talk or play with her (at about two months)

Three Months to One Year

- Watches faces with interest and follows moving objects
- Recognizes familiar objects and people; smiles at the sound of your voice
- Begins to develop a social smile
- Turns toward sounds

One to Two Years

- Explores his environment; gets into things
- Takes one long nap a day
- Plays alone for short periods of time
- Explores his body
- Often seems to be out of step with the world
- Can be oppositional – for example, when asked to come, will move away
- Seldom obeys a verbal command. Favorite word is "No."
- Not easily motivated by words
- Impatient in the extreme. Can't wait and only understands "Now."

- Has problems giving to others and may treat people, except parents, as objects
- Although his language is limited, he understands more words than he can say.
- Can walk, run, and sometimes climb, but his balance is very unsteady
- Has a quick temper and is emotionally very immature

Two Years

- More mature and calm and is willing to do more of the things she can do
- Runs, climbs, pushes, pulls and is very active; more sure of her motor skills
- Can communicate more effectively and make her wants known
- Can feed herself with fingers, spoon, and cup
- Life is easier emotionally. Demands are not as strong and can wait a moment if necessary.
- Is more interested in people and occasionally likes to please
- Can remove some of her clothing
- Explores her genitalia
- Sleeps less and wakes easily
- Thrives on routines
- Becomes upset if her mother is away overnight
- Is balky and indecisive; changes her mind
- Imitates adults
- Cannot share with other children
- Plays beside but not with children her own age
- Is often loving, affectionate, and warmly responsive to others
- Likes water play

- Prolongs the good-night ritual

Three Years

- Runs, jumps, and climbs
- Feeds himself; drinks neatly from a cup
- Carries things without spilling
- Can help dress and undress himself
- May not sleep at naptime but plays quietly
- Is responsive to adults; wants approval
- Is sensitive to expressions of disapproval
- Cooperates; likes to run simple errands
- Is at a "Me too!" stage; wants to be included
- Is curious about things and people
- Is imaginative; may fear the dark or animals
- May have an imaginary companion
- May get out of bed at night
- Is talkative; uses short sentences
- Can't wait his turn; has little patience
- Can take some responsibility, such as for putting toys away
- Plays well alone, but group play can be stormy
- Is attached to the parent of the opposite sex
- Is jealous, especially of a new baby
- Demonstrates guilt feelings
- Releases emotional insecurity by whining, crying, or requesting reassurances of love
- Releases tension by thumbsucking and nail biting

Four Years

- Continues to gain weight and height
- Continues to gain coordination

- Has good eating, sleeping, and elimination habits
- Is very active
- Starts things but doesn't necessarily finish them
- Is bossy or boastful
- Plays with others but is self-assertive
- Has short-lived quarrels
- Speaks clearly; is a great talker
- Tells stories and exaggerates
- Uses toilet words in a silly way
- Makes up meaningless words with loss of syllables
- Laughs and giggles
- Dawdles
- Washes when told
- Is at the "How and why?" stage
- Demonstrates dependence on peers

Five Years

- Can be an angel at this age, which is a time of extreme and delightful stability
- Is generally reliable, stable, and well adjusted
- Feels secure within herself; is calm, friendly, and generally not demanding of others
- Generally does not want to go into the unknown
- Is usually successful in what she tries to do but only tries what she can accomplish
- Likes to be near mother, do things with and for her, and obey her commands
- Seeks to be a "good" child, which is something that she usually can accomplish
- Good behavior ends around 5½ to 6, leaving parents wishing their nice 5-year-old were back.

Six Years

- The child is extremely difficult to deal with.
- Much like a two-and-a-half-year-old, he is violently emotional – loving one minute and hating the next.
- Mother is no longer as important. He becomes the center of his own universe, with mother now blamed for all that is momentarily wrong.
- As when he was two and a half, he is very demanding of others and very rigid in his demands.
- Extremely negative in his response to others and refuses to do what he is asked simply because he was asked
- Has great energy
- Has problems deciding between two options because he wants both
- Cannot accept criticism, blame, and punishment. He has to always be right, win, and be praised.
- Is rigid and unadaptable in relations with others, just as he was at two and a half. This leads to tears and accusations that others are cheating if he doesn't win.
- As long as all goes well, he can be warm, enthusiastic, eager, and ready for anything new.

Seven Years

- Withdraws from the world and likes to be alone with her own things
- Is much calmer than her six-year-old self and is easier to live with
- Is more likely to complain than to rejoice
- Tends to mope and may be described as morose and moody
- Likes to watch, listen, and stay on the edge of any activity

- Wants to touch and feel everything she comes in contact with
- Plays with her intellect more
- Often demands too much of herself
- Has good days and bad days, days she learns well, and days she forgets everything
- Often feels people are against her, don't like her, and are picking on her
- Uses facial expressions and frequent pouting to express dissatisfaction with life
- Good days will steadily increase until she is ready for most anything by eight years of age.

Eight Years

- Often described as expansive and speedy; goes out to meet the world
- Believes nothing is too difficult for him
- Tends to meet new and difficult challenges with great excitement
- Enjoys new experiences, trying out new things, and making new friends
- Often overestimates his own ability follow through, sometimes leading to failure and becoming discouraged; needs help to better plan for tasks
- Frequent failures are met with tears and self-disparagement: "I always do it wrong," and "I never get anything right."
- Failures today will not stop him from starting something new tomorrow.
- Interested in two-way relationships with people and is concerned about them and wants to know what they think

- Has more to say to other people and expects more of them as well
- Wants and demands a close, understanding relationship with his mother
- Brash and brave, but much more sensitive than expected
- Gives a hint of the person he will become

Appendix II

Childproofing Checklist

Alarming statistics show that accidents constitute the number one cause of death in young children. Most accidents occur as a result of children's normal, healthy curiosity. Chances of getting hurt increase as children creep, crawl, walk, climb, and explore.

The following checklist identifies steps parents and everyone on the parenting team should take to prevent accidents at their home or preschool/daycare:

- Always keep guns and knives locked safely away from children. Each gun should have its own trigger lock, and ammunition should be locked in a separate location out of reach of little hands.
- Install childproof latches on all cabinets and drawers that contain dangerous objects.
- Crawl through the house on your hands and knees to spot enticing hazards to be remedied.
- Plug empty electrical outlets with plastic plugs designed for this purpose.
- Remove unused extension cords.

- Move large pieces of furniture in front of electrical outlets that have cords plugged into them, or install protective outlet coverings that prevent a child from unplugging the cord.
- If small tables or other furnishings are not sturdy or have sharp corners, put them away until your child is older or install protective coverings on sharp edges.
- If there are large pieces of furniture that a child can climb and tip over, secure them to a nearby wall.
- Place dangerous household substances – such as detergents, cleaning fluids, razor blades, matches, and medicines – well out of reach in a locked cabinet.
- Install a proper screen on a fireplace.
- Always use a correct car seat in your automobile.
- Regularly check toys for sharp edges or small broken pieces.
- Check the floor for small objects that your child could swallow or choke on.
- Put a gate on a stairway to prevent unsupervised play on the stairs.
- Never leave your baby unattended on a changing table, in the bathtub, on a couch, on your bed, in an infant seat or highchair, on the floor, or in a car.
- Place small, fragile tabletop items out of your child's reach.
- Keep the door to the bathroom closed at all times. Use a childproof doorknob cover if your child knows how to turn the doorknob.
- Install safety latches on toilet lids.
- Keep plastic bags and small objects (pins, buttons, nuts, hard candy, and money) out of reach at all times.
- Make sure toys, furniture, and walls are finished in lead-free paint. Check labels to make sure toys are nontoxic.
- Teach the word *hot* as early as you can. Keep your child away from the hot oven, iron, vent, fireplace, wood stove,

barbecue grill, cigarettes, cigarette lighter, teacups, and coffee cups.

- Always turn pot handles inward when cooking and remove gas knobs from the stove when not in use.
- Install safety latches for stand-alone freezers and oven doors, if they don't have locks.
- Do not hang a tablecloth off a table when your small child is close by.
- Never tie toys to a crib or playpen. Your baby could strangle on the string. Also, never attach a pacifier to a string that could get wrapped around your baby's neck.

Appendix III

Is My Child Hyperactive?

If you suspect that your young child is hyperactive, the following guidelines will help you know what to expect when his behavior is evaluated. Only a detailed picture of your child and how he navigates his world can lead to an appropriate diagnosis and an effective treatment plan. When conducting a thorough evaluation, a trained mental health professional (a psychologist, social worker, or psychiatrist) will gather information in the following areas:

A. Family history, including the following:

1. Your child's developmental, school, and treatment history
2. Your family's psychiatric history
3. All previous diagnostic screenings done on your child
4. Behavior checklists completed by parents, teachers, and so on
5. Your child's social functioning at home, in the neighborhood, and at school
6. How your family understands and reacts to your child's behavior
7. Your child's sleep patterns
8. Your child's diet and allergies

9. An analysis of the factors related to your child's behavior, including the following:
   a. How your child interacts with his mother, father, siblings, peers, teachers, coaches, and so on
   b. How your child reacts at home, in school, at social gatherings, in the neighborhood, and so on
   c. How your child reacts to reading, writing, homework, video games, getting dressed, and so on
   d. How your child behaves early in the morning, after school, during meals, when he's bored, at bedtime, and so on

B. An interview with your child to gather the following information:

1. His understanding of and thoughts about his problems
2. His general emotional functioning

C. An analysis of your child's behavior in school, including the following:

1. Teacher-completed behavioral checklists
2. Teachers' understanding of and reaction to your child's behavior
3. Classroom observation of your child across several tasks and settings

D. Formal testing to evaluate the following:

1. General cognitive functioning
2. Achievement skills
3. Attention to tasks
4. Language processing
5. Sensory-motor skills

Appendix IV

The ACE Study by Vincent Felitti and Robert Anda

http: //www.cdc.gov/violenceprevention/acestudy/

This study is one of the largest investigations ever conducted to assess associations between childhood maltreatment and later-life health and well-being. The study is a collaboration between the Centers for Disease Control and Prevention and Kaiser Permanente's Health Appraisal Clinic in San Diego.

More than 17,000 Health Maintenance Organization (HMO) members undergoing a comprehensive physical examination chose to provide detailed information about their childhood experience of abuse, neglect, and family dysfunction. The questionnaires, which were collected from 1995 to 1997, sampled a middle-class to upper-middle-class demographic.

To date, more than 50 scientific articles have been published and more than 100 conference and workshop presentations have been made. Overall, the ACE Study findings suggest that certain experiences are major risk factors for the leading causes of illness and death, as well as poor quality of life, in the United States.

The high frequency of adverse experiences among the generally well-to-do population in the study surprised the researchers. In addition, Anda was quoted saying in the book *How Children Succeed,* "The correlations between adverse childhood experiences and negative adult outcomes were so powerful that they stunned us."

The more adverse experiences in childhood, the greater the likelihood of developmental delays and later health problems – including heart disease, diabetes, substance abuse, and depression.

NOTE:

The ACE Study, National Public Radio, All Things Considered, March 2, 2015 http://www.npr.org/player/v2/mediaPlayer.html?action=l&t=3&islist=true&id=2&d=03-02-2015/

JAICO PUBLISHING HOUSE

Elevate Your Life. Transform Your World.

ESTABLISHED IN 1946, Jaico Publishing House is home to world-transforming authors such as Robin Sharma, Sadhguru, Osho, the Dalai Lama, Deepak Chopra, Eknath Easwaran, Paramhansa Yogananda, Devdutt Pattanaik, Radhakrishnan Pillai, Morgan Housel, Napoleon Hill, John Maxwell, Brian Tracy, and Stephen Hawking.

Our late founder Mr. Jaman Shah first established Jaico as a book distribution company. Sensing that independence was around the corner, he aptly named his company Jaico ('Jai' means victory in Hindi). In order to service the significant demand for affordable books in a developing nation, Mr. Shah initiated Jaico's own publications. Jaico was India's first publisher of paperback books in the English language.

While self-help; religion and philosophy; mind, body and spirit; and business titles form the cornerstone of our non-fiction list, we publish an exciting range of current affairs, history, biography, art and architecture, travel, and popular science books as well. Our renewed focus on popular fiction is evident in our new titles by a host of fresh young talent from India and abroad.

Jaico's translations division publishes select bestselling titles in over 10 regional languages including Gujarati, Hindi, Kannada, Malayalam, Marathi, Tamil, and Telugu. These include titles from renowned national and international authors like Sudha Murthy, Gaur Gopal Das, Swami Mukundananda, Jay Shetty, Simon Sinek, Ankur Warikoo and Jeff Keller.

Visit our Website

Boasting one of India's largest book distribution networks, Jaico has its headquarters in Mumbai, with branches in Ahmedabad, Bangalore, Chennai, Delhi, Hyderabad, and Kolkata. This network ensures that our books reach all parts of the country, both urban and rural.